A JOURNEY OF RICHES

Transformational Change

11 Insights to strengthen your resolve

A Journey Of Riches - Transformational Change
11 Insights to strengthen your resolve © 2018
Spender, John

Copyright © 2018 John Spender

This work is copyright. Apart from any use as permitted under the Copyright Act 1968, no part may be reproduced, copied, scanned, stored in a retrieval system, recorded or transmitted, in any form or by any means, without the prior permission of the publisher.

The rights of John Spender to be identified as the primary author of this work has been asserted by him under the Copyright Amendment (Moral Rights) Act 2000 Disclaimer.

The author and publishers have used their best efforts in preparing this book and disclaim liability arising directly and indirectly, consequential or otherwise from its contents.

All reasonable efforts have been made to obtain necessary copyright permissions. Any omissions or errors are unintentional and will, if brought to the attention of the publishers, be corrected in future impressions and printings.

Published by Motion Media International
Editing: Gwendolyn Parker, Chris Drabenstott.
Cover Design: Motion Media International
Typesetting & Assembly: Motion Media International
Printing: Create Space

Creator: Spender, John - Primary Author
Title: *A Journey Of Riches - Transformational Change*
11 Insights to strengthen your resolve
ISBN Print: 978-0-6482845-5-0
ISBN Digital: 978-0-6482845-6-7
Subjects: Self-Help, Motivation/Inspiration and Spirituality.

Acknowledgements

Reading and writing is a gift that too few give to themselves, it is such a powerful way to reflect and gain closure from the past, reading and writing is a therapeutic process. The experience raises ones self-esteem, confidence and awareness of self.

I learned this when I created the first book in the *A Journey Of Riches* series, which is, now one of twelve books with over 130 different co-authors from twenty two different countries. It's not easy to write about your own personal experience's and I honor and respect everyone of the authors who has collaborated in the series thus far. For many of the authors, English is their second language, which is a major achievement within its self.

In curating this anthology of short stories, I have felt such incredible challenge, joy, and I have been inspired by the amount of generosity, gratitude, and shared energy that this experience has given everyone.

The idea for this book came from Mia Tolis the author of chapter six while we were chatting about collaborating together. Initially Mia was going to write in book nine *Transformation Calling* but was unable to make the due date, because of a heavy influx of work commitments. I'm honoured to be co-authoring this book with Mia and nine other inspiring authors from around the world. It is our hope that this book will strengthen your spirit to face your life and to make it truly epic. Here it is book 12 in the *A Journey Of Riches* series Transformational Change, *11 Insights to strengthen your resolve.*

Of course, I could not have created this book without the ten other co-authors who each said YES when I asked them to share their insights into how they found and find inspiration in their life. Just like each chapter in this book makes for inspiring reading, each story represents one chapter in the life of each of the authors, with the chief aim of having you, the reader, living a more fulfilling life.

I'd like to thank all the authors for entrusting me with their unique memories, encounters and wisdom. Thank you for sharing and opening the door to your soul, so others may learn from your experience, may the readers gleam confidence from your success's and wisdom from your failures.

Thank you to my family, I know you are proud of me and how far I have come from that 10 year old boy who was just learning how to read and write at a basic level. Mom, Robert, Dad, Merril, my brother Adam and his daughter Krystal, my sister Hollie, her partner Brian, my nephew Charlie and my niece Heidi. Also my grandparents Gran and Pop who are alive and well and Ma and Pa who now resting in peace. They accept me just the way I am with all my travels and adventures around the world.

Thanks to all the team at MotionMediaInternational who have done an excellent job at editing and collating this book. It has been a pleasure working with you all on this successful project, and I thank you for your patience in dealing with the various changes and adjustments along the way.

Thank you, the reader for having the courage to look at your life and how you can improve your future in a fast and rapidly changing world.

And I'd enjoy to connect with readers, as I love sharing stories.

You can email me here: jrspender7@gmail.com

Thank you again to my fellow co-authors: John Hanna, JoJo Bennington, Tracy Sotirakis, Tom Wind, Mia Tolis, Elli Petrovska, Kim Joss, Stephen Smith, Sandy Escabi, Nikki Galagher.

I hope you have enjoyed, this co-authored experience as much as I have. Love and light.

Praise

"If you are looking for an inspiring read to get you through any change, this is it!! This book is filled with many gripping perspectives, from a collection of successful international authors with a tonne of wisdom to share."
~ Theera Phetmalaigul, Entrepreneur/Investor.

"*A Journey Of Riches* is an empowering series that implements two simple words in overcoming life's struggles.
By diving into the meaning of the words "problem" and "challenge," you will find yourself motivated to believe in the triumph of perseverance. With many different authors from all around the world, coming together to share different stories of life's trials, you will find yourself drenched in encouragement to push through even the darkest of battles.
The stories are personal heart felt shares of moving through and transforming challenges into rich life experiences.
The book will move, touch and inspire your spirit to face and overcome any of life's adversities. A truly inspirational read. Thank you for being the kind open soul you are John!!"
~ Casey Plouffe, Seven Figure Network Marketer.

"A must read for anyone facing major changes or challenges in life right now. This book will give you the courage to move through any challenge with confidence, grace and ease."
~ Jo-Anne Irwin - Transformational Coach & Best Selling Author.

"I'm a fan of self-help books and I read them a lot. I love this book and the stories that are contained within them, but most of all I love the concept. I love that John Spender decided to do an anthology of stories from inspirational people. This is the type of book where you can either choose to be inspired by 10 different stories or choose a chapter that resonates with you the most.
As I read this book, it confirmed to me my life suspicion that things happen in our lives we can't control. It can be extremely devastating at times. It is those moments that bring us to our knees not knowing whether we can or even want to stand anymore. But, in these challenging moments, this book confirms to me that we do have one choice we can let go, make changes and embrace the new. It's the choice of how we decide to view these hardships. Our perspective determines what our life will be after these moments in our lives.
There were some very heart wrenching stories that were contained in these books. Some of them I even had to ask myself, "How do you even recover from a situation like that?"

Perspective. It all boils down to how we decide to view those hard challenges that come our way. At least that is what I took away from this book.
Thank you to John and his team of authors for getting together to create this book."
~ Kit Zakimi on Amazon.

"I have really enjoyed the Journey of Riches book series. Each person's story is written from the heart and everyone's personal journey different. We all have a story to tell and John Spender does an amazing job of finding authors and combining their stories, into uplifting books."
~ Liz Misner Palmer, Foreign Service Officer.

"A timely read as I'm facing a few changes right now. I liked the various insights from the different authors.This book will inspire you to move through any challenge or change that you are experiencing."
~ David Ostrand, Business Owner.

"I've known John Spender for a while now, I was blessed with an opportunity to be in book four in the series. I know that you will enjoy this new journey like the rest of the books in the series. The collection of stories will assist you with making changes, to deal with challenges and to see that transformation is possible for your life."
~Charlie O'shea, Entrepreneur.

"*A Journey of Riches* series will draw you in and help you dig deep into your soul. Every author has an unbelievable life story of purpose inside of them. John Spender is dedicated to bringing peace, love and adventure to the world of his readers! Dive into this series and you will be transformed!!"
~ Jeana Matichak, Author of Finding Peace.

"Awesome! Truly inspirational! It is amazing what the human spirit can achieve and overcome! Highly recommended!!"
~Fabrice Beliard, Australian Business Coach and Best Selling Author.

"*A Journey of Riches Series* is a must read. It is an empowering collection of inspirational and moving stories full of courage, strength and heart. Bringing peace and awareness to those lucky enough to read to assist and inspire them on their own life journey."
~Gemma Castiglia, Avalon Healing, Best Selling Author.

"The *A Journey of Riches* book series is a inspirational collection of books that will empower you to take on any challenge or change in life."
~Kay Newton, Midlife Stress Buster and Best Selling Author.

"*A Journey of Riches* book series are an inspiring collection of stories, sharing many different ideas and perspectives on how to overcome challenges, deal with change and to make empowering choices in your life. Open the book anywhere and let your mood chose where you need to read. Buy one of the books today, you'll be glad that you did! "
~Trish Rock, Modern Day Intuitive, Best selling Author, Speaker, Psychic & Holistic Coach.

"*Transformational Change* is another inspiring read in the *A Journey of Riches* book series. The authors are from all over the world and each has a unique perspective to share, that will have you thinking differently about you're current circumstances in life. An inspiring read!"
~Alexandria Calamel, Success Coach and Best Selling Author.

"The *A Journey of Riches* books are a collection of real life stories, that are truly inspiring and give you the confidence that no matter what you are dealing with in your life, that there is a light at the end of the tunnel, and a very bright one at that.
Totally empowering!"
~ John Abbott, Freedom Entrepreneur.

"An amazing collection of true stories from individuals who have overcome great changes and who have transformed their lives and use their experience to uplift, inspire and support others."
~Carol Williams, Author-Speaker-Coach.

"You can empower yourself from the power within this book, that can help awaken the sleeping giant within you. John has a purpose in life to bring inspiring people together to share their wisdom, for the benefit of all who venture deep into this book *Transformational Change*. If you are looking for inspiration to be someone special this book can be your guide."
~Bill Bilwani, Renown Melbourne Restaurateur.

"In *A Journey Of Riches: Transformational Change*, the twelfth book in the series, you will again catch the impulse to step up, reconsider and settle for only the very best for yourself and those around you. Penned from the heart and with an unflinching drive to make a difference for the good of all, *A Journey Of Riches* series is a must-read."
~Steve Coleman Author of *"Decisions, Decisions! How to Make the Right One Every Time."*

"If you want to be on top of your game? *A Journey of Riches* is a must read with breakthrough insights that will help you do just that!"
~ Christopher Chen, Entrepreneur.

"In *A Journey of Riches*, you will find the insight, resources and tools you need to transform your life. By reading the authors stories, you too can be inspired to achieve your greatest accomplishments and what is truly possible for you. Reading this book activates your true potential for transforming, you're life way beyond what you think is possible. Read it and learn how you too can have a magical life."
~Elaine Mc Guinness, Best selling Author of *Unleash Your Authentic Self!*

"If you are looking for an inspiring read look no further than the *A Journey Of Riches* book series. The books are an inspiring collection of short stories, that will encourage you to embrace life even more. I highly recommend you read one of the books today!"
~Kara Dono, Doula, Healer and Best Selling Author.

"*A Journey of Riches* series is a must read for anyone seeking to enrich their own lives and gain wisdom through the wonderful stories of personal empowerment & triumphs over life's challenges. I've given several copies to my family, friends and clients to inspire and support them to step into their greatness. I highly recommend that you read these books, savoring the many aha's and tools you will discover inside."
~Michele Cempaka, Hypnotherapist, Shaman, Transformational Coach & Reiki Master.

"If you are looking for an inspirational read, look no further than the *A Journey Of Riches* book series. The books are an inspiring and educational collection of short stories from the authors soul itself, that will encourage you to embrace life even more. I've even given them to my clients too, so that they are inspired with their journeys in life, wealth, health and everything else in between.
I recommend you make it a priority, to read one of the books today!"
~Goro Gupta, Chief Education Officer, Mortgage Terminator, Property Mentor.

"The *A Journey Of Riches* book series is filled with real-life short stories of heartfelt tribulations turned into uplifting, self-transformation by the power of the human spirit to overcome adversity. The journeys captured in these books will encourage you to embrace life in a whole new way.
I highly recommend reading this inspiring anthology series."
~Chris Drabenstott, Best Selling Author and Editor.

"There is so much motivational power in the *A Journey of Riches* series!! Each book is a compilation of inspiring, real-life stories by several different authors, which makes the journey feel more relatable and success more attainable. If you are looking for something to move you forward, you'll find it in one (or all) of these books."
~Cary Mac Arthur, Personal Empowerment Coach

"I've been fortunate to write with John Spender and now call him a friend. *A Journey of Riches* book series features real stories that have inspired me and will inspire you. John has a passion for finding amazing people from all of the world, giving the series a global perspective on important subject matters."

~Mike Campbell, Fat Guy Diary, LLC

Table of Contents

Introduction 17

CHAPTER ONE
An Unlikely Transformation
By John Spender 21

CHAPTER TWO
The Running Man
By John Hanna *(with Timothy Marlowe)* 37

CHAPTER THREE
Dare to Redefine Yourself
By JoJo Bennington 65

CHAPTER FOUR
The Power Of Asking
By Tracy Sotirakis 89

CHAPTER FIVE
Ultimate Healing
By Tom Wind 103

CHAPTER SIX
The Presents in Presence
By Mia Tolis 129

CHAPTER SEVEN
Transitional Change
By Stephen R. Smith 155

CHAPTER EIGHT
Heal Your SoulSelf
By Kim Joss.. 169

CHAPTER NINE
Transformation
By Elli Petrovska 187

CHAPTER TEN
Passion Drives A New Beginning
By Sandy Escabi.. 207

CHAPTER ELEVEN
From Sick And Tired to Healthy And Wealthy
By Nikki Galagher.. 223

Author Biographies... 245

Afterword.. 267

Introduction

I created this book and chose the different authors to share their personal insights, wisdom, and experiences to assist people who may be going through challenges, adversities, or changes similar to those of the authors.

Like all of us, each author has a unique story and insight to share with you. It just may be the case, that one or more of these authors have lived through an experience that is similar to circumstances in life right now. Their words could be just the words you need to read to help you through your challenges. Perhaps reading about one or more of these experiences will fill in the missing piece of your puzzle, so to speak, allowing you to move forward into the next phase on your journey.

Storytelling has been the way humankind has communicated ideas and learning throughout our civilization. While we have become more sophisticated, and life in the modern world is more convenient, there is still much discontent and dissatisfaction with one's reality. Many people have also moved away from reading books, and they are missing out on valuable information that can help them to move forward in life, with a positive outlook. I think it is important to turn off the T.V., to slow down, and to read, reflect, and take the time to appreciate everything you have in life.

I like anthology books because they carry many different perspectives and insights on a singular topic. I find that sometimes when I'm reading a book that has just one author I gain an understanding of their perspective and writing style very quickly and the reading becomes predicable. With this book and all of the books in the *A Journey of Riches* book series, you have many different writing styles and viewpoints that will help shape your own perspective towards your current set of circumstances.

Anthology books are also great because you can start from any chapter and gain a valuable insight or a nugget of wisdom without the feeling that you have missed something from the earlier chapters.

I love reading many different types of personal development books, because learning and personal growth is important to me. If you are not learning and growing, well, you're staying the same. Everything in the universe is growing, expanding, and changing. If we are not open to different ideas and different ways of thinking and being, then we can become close-minded.

The idea of this book series is to open you up to different ways of perceiving your reality, to give you hope, to give you encouragement, and to give you many avenues of thinking about the same subject. My wish for you, is to feel empowered to make a decision that will best suit you in moving forward with your life. As Albert Einstein said, "We cannot solve problems with the same level of thinking that created them."

With Einstein's words in mind, let your mood pick a chapter in the book and allow yourself to be guided to find the answers you seek.

"Emotion is the chef source of all becoming conscious.

There can be no transforming of darkness into light

and of apathy into movement without emotion."

~ Carl Jung

CHAPTER ONE

An Unlikely Transformation

By John Spender

It was the year 2000, the new millennium. The year that was meant to begin with a hurricane-like disaster as a result of the Y2K computer bug, the year of the Sydney Olympics touted as the best ever by many Olympic committee members, and the year I dumped my friend, cocaine, only to regularly welcome depression and anxiety into my life.

It wasn't all doom and gloom, though. I moved into a new house on the North Shore of Sydney in Lane Cove. I transitioned from my landscape gardening business into a state sales representative position for a textile company that had the licence for Biggie Best in Australia, a position that I would struggle with, as the rejection at the time was too much for me to handle. It was the year where I tried many things as my old world died and a new world was opening up to me.

I tried boxing, and I had my first amateur match and won, but I didn't like hurting people, so I quit. I was seeing a counsellor for a while, but I found it hard to open up and I didn't really get any results. I tried anti-depressants, but that made me feel terrible and I felt void of any emotion. Looking back now, I can see that I was a dabbler with little or no confidence, and it was another two years regularly doing depression before I discovered international travel and my first serious relationship. She was the first girl that I lived with and the first relationship that lasted more than four months.

In those two years, I spent way too much time with anxiety and depression. Have you ever felt confused, not sure what to do next? Well, that was mostly my life for two years. As a dabbler, meant I didn't have any commitment or resolve to stick with one thing. In those two years, my life was on repeat, and I found sales to be such a difficult challenge. I went through four sales jobs in four years, and I was sacked from all of them except one. My transformation has taken place over a long period of time.

In my experience, transformation is a process of evolving over a period of time. Sometimes it can feel like you are going backwards, but that back step can be moving you further forward. Almost like firing an arrow at a target, first the arrow goes backwards before it shoots forward. Like all the experiences and stories I share in the *A*

Journey of Riches book series, this is just a snippet of my life shared in the hope that it will make your journey a bit easier. When you summon the courage to pursue a worthwhile vision consistently, your life will truly change into something deliberate and magical.

Now back to this period in my life that was a stepping stone to the magical life that I live today.

The first job after moving on from my business was with Mahogany Textiles, the company that had the Australian licence for Biggie Best Fabrics, similar to the Laura Ashely range. This was a huge challenge for me, going from landscape to fabric sales. I knew nothing about curtain, furniture, or bedding fabric, and here I was travelling the state of NSW introducing a new range to the market. It was challenging, not only because of the consistent rejection, but I had to convince interior designers to buy our exclusive sample range when most of the competitors gave their samples away for free. I made a few sales, but not as many as my boss expected. Phil had been a gardening client of mine before he offered me a job with his new venture. My second review after a six-month stint and lacklustre results, Phil sat me down on a Monday morning after I crashed the company van into a ditch while drink driving. It was clear to both of us that I was experiencing a crisis in confidence, and it was best that I found employment elsewhere.

The second job was selling Optus landline and internet packages door to door on 100% commission, and after a terrible first month where I made no sales, I'd used all the little savings that I had, and my meals were very basic. Finally, on a field trip to Tamworth, I cracked it and my spiel clicked, and I made a whopping 19 sales in one day, zero to hero. This was just the spike in confidence that I needed. I went on to become a manager. Each day was a challenge to motivate myself to take the team around residential streets to knock on doors. Also, I didn't like the fact that I couldn't take the van home. I decided to casually see if I could find a higher paying job, and I found one, applied, aced the interview, and got the job with a company car, a base rate, and healthy commissions.

Here I was in my third job in just 12 months, and it wasn't like I was working and travelling. I was trying to make an honest living. The third job, I was selling indoor plants to big corporate companies and, given my experience in horticulture and owning my own landscape gardening business for five years, I thought I would take to it like a duck to water. I was reasonably confident, from my experience selling door to door, but selling to corporates was much harder than I'd anticipated. With door-to-door sales, if someone answered the door, nine times out of ten it would be the decision-maker, the person who would make the purchase, right? The trick with door-to-door sales was to make a solid first impression, and I did this by flashing a broad smile, looking into their eyes as if we had met somewhere before, and with an excellent offer and quick rebuttals to any objections. It was quite easy. In the new sales position, my title was sales executive of new business, which was just another fancy word for cold calling. Cold calling on corporations was a lot more challenging for me. First of all, you had to get past, or charm, the receptionist, even to get a glance at a decision-maker. Most of the time, you would receive a business card and be asked to email them your prices. And what made it harder was the fact that we weren't allowed to leave a display sample with them.

The displays the company had were amazing, and we gave a high level of service after they were installed; these were the positives. The company was the most expensive on the market, and the sales manager was asking us to do dodgy things like placing our hands over the install fee as we had them to sign a two-year contract. The company had these outrageously expensive plastic flower arrangements, although they did look real. One particular HR manager of a large RSL Club liked the flower arrangements. I sold her five arrangements per week for two years at $50 each. She signed the contract and we sent the delivery. It wasn't until she did the maths that she realised that was $26,000. She wanted to cancel the order, and I thought that was fair enough since they'd only had them for a few days. The company wanted to enforce the contract, and quite often they did this kind of thing, as they were a large multi-national company with a strong team of in-house lawyers just for this type of situation. The more I worked for the company, the more I realised how dodgy they were, and I didn't feel comfortable working for them.

The way we signed clients up did change, and our team environment began to change to a positive one. I wasn't happy, most of the time doing depression, and I would also have epic panic attacks. Even though I wasn't getting many sales, neither were any of the other sales reps. When I had a bad day or week and wanted to quit, my manager would take me out for dinner and we'd get blind drunk. On one particular occasion, he let me drive his sports car and I sped off at the lights, and right behind me was an unmarked cop car. I blew high range and was forced to take a cab home. The manager, of course, kept this under wraps, and he helped me find a barrister—which was two thousand dollars in 2001—who somehow managed to convince the judge to drop the charges on the provision that I complete a six-week anti-drink-driving program. It was an intense and confronting program in which we met victims of drink-driving accidents. One of them was a paraplegic, and he shared with us all the gory details. It was an uncomfortable experience. I felt lucky that I didn't cause an accident or destroy someone's life. We had assignments where we had to make a report on a nasty accident, and they showed us photos of the victims, another uncomfortable experience. It was a difficult and expensive lessen to learn, but I showed up every week and completed the program when many didn't.

It was like I was trying to sabotage myself in the hope of getting fired. In another incident, the company put on a weekend event for all the sales staff, and we went out the night before the team-building day. I didn't know how to manage my anxiety, so I drank like a fish and ate like a pig to repress my uncomfortable feelings. I ended up in some night club in Kings Cross where an old clubbing buddy gave me an ecstasy pill and we partied all night. I went straight from the club to my hotel room, had a shower, got changed, and went to the meeting point. We had been booked on a yachting trip around Sydney Harbour. I was off my chops, behaving loudly and obnoxiously. Many of the reps and the sales manager couldn't get out of bed because they were hung over. The branch manager was there, and he wasn't impressed. It was quite clear that I was on something other than alcohol, and I had my prize trip that I had won to the Sunshine Coast taken away from me. I then took three days off work and drank myself sober, and I still couldn't get fired.

I did have a few big wins, including signing the offices of Ford up to a $93,000 yearly contract, but I was mostly inconsistent with my sales. My sales would match my mood, which was manic and up and down like a yo-yo.

One week would be incredible and the atmosphere at the office would be buzzing. The next, I would be lucky to get one sale, and I was miserable to be around. I did reduce my drinking during the week. I became a member of a health club, and the exercise before and after work helped me to maintain a level of sanity. I started to apply for other sales jobs while still selling indoor plant hire. I was at a convention for pubs and clubs, as we had a stand there. I was generating some solid leads; I was having an up day. The problem was, they had these cute girls offering free shots of some new alcohol, and then I was invited to the bar at the venue with a potential client. Next thing I knew, I'd had more than a few drinks. They shut the bar and I sneaked behind and grabbed a Sub Zero out of the fridge, and someone told on me.

I had the sense to get out of there and catch a train home, but this big bouncer came after me. He grabbed me and tried to take me back to the bar. Instinctively, I swivelled out of his grip and gave him a left hook to his chin and dropped him. I legged it out of there, but in the scuffle my name tag had dropped off my shirt. The next day, I got called into my manager's office. He sternly explained that everyone in the company knew what I'd done the previous evening. He wanted my version of the story, and I told him everything. I was given a written warning and then we went back to the venue so I could apologise to the bouncer. When we arrived, he was sitting at a bar table with three other guys drinking beers at about 12 o'clock. As we got closer, you could see that he was a big unit, even sitting down. I said I was sorry. He was red-faced and mumbled something. He didn't even look me in the eye. I saw that he had a bunch of stitches in his mouth. His drinking buddies were speechless. They had looks on their faces like, *What the fuck? You got dropped by that tall lanky guy? Are you serious?*

My manager wasn't happy, mostly because the general manager was giving him grief. I was finally going to get the sack. The following week, I had two interviews, one with the general manager about my position with the company and the other one with the general manager of Fitness First, the new club opening on Pitt Street in the city. The first interview didn't go too well, and I was fired. (The GM used the term "let go.") He told me he was going to pay me for the rest of the month, which was two weeks. He said I should grab my things and leave immediately and that he wished me all the best for my future. The second interview went really well, and I aced it. The fact that I was already a member and had sales experience worked in my favour. I started the following week, and I was excited for the new opportunity.

In the beginning the role wasn't very exciting. The club wasn't quite finished, and we were pre-selling memberships, which meant visiting the corporations and the local shops and handing out leaflets to people walking past, offering them a discounted membership. It was a good company to work for, not only for the perks of a free membership and a half-priced membership for two friends or family. The environment was competitive. There was a strong emphasis on personal development, and they provided training programs to help us to be at our best. Each day there was a minimum activity requirement that we had to meet. They had an effective sales system by which they could predict that, if you made thirty calls and booked four appointments, you could expect to make at least two sales a day. The expectation that you would achieve your daily targets was too much for many people, and I saw consultants who only lasted a day before they quit. The turnover of sales staff was also high. In addition to daily targets, we also had to generate our own leads, which meant lots of cold calling. I generally like meeting people. The best leads were walk-ins, people who intentionally go into the health club to inquire about membership. The chances of selling a membership to a walk-in was high.

On a deeper level, I wasn't very happy, and I didn't have a sense of who I was or what I wanted. At the end-of-year Christmas party, it became clear that I yearned for a girlfriend. The party was at Fox Sports Bar at Moore Park just outside the city. The night started with rounds of shots with our sales team. As it was free booze, I made the most of it. To say I became quite drunk is an understatement. I'd even had a juicy hamburger before the party, but it didn't make much of a difference. One of the other membership consultants, Oscar from Mosman, a big friendly giant and well liked. He had this beautiful girlfriend with him. I don't remember her name, but I remember the chemistry they had together. It was electrifying to me, and I knew that's what I wanted. The rest of the night was a bit of a blur, but somehow I got into a fight with Oscar out front of the venue. The next day, I couldn't work out what had happened. Why would I fight with such a nice guy? As the shattered pieces of the night before came together, I worked out that I was jealous of him and what he had. Naturally, I apologised to him, and he just shook it off as if nothing had happened, but I felt so bad for weeks afterwards. He was the type of person that I wanted to be like; I just didn't know how to make that happen, and it made me sad.

It wasn't until I met my then-girlfriend, Pavlina, that I started to express myself, experience a broader spectrum of emotions, and to feel genuinely happy. Having a partner gave me a deeper sense of connection and someone with whom to explore and do things for the first time.

She was from the Czech Republic and was in Australia on a student visa. She was 32 and I was 25. We met when I signed her friend up on a 12-month gym membership, after she flirted with me, fluttering her eye lids like a butterfly, giggling and constantly blushing. I signed her friend up right on closing, and my buddy was waiting for me, and we went on a double date of sorts. It didn't last long, though, because Pavlina's friend didn't like my friend and she wanted to go home.

After a couple of dates, she told me that she was in an unhappy marriage and she was still living with her husband. I was disappointed, to say the least. However, she kept sending me text messages, and we continued seeing each other. I soon helped her move down the road from my place before she eventually moved in with me. In the summer of '02, we went to visit Czech Republic to meet her family for three weeks, and it was a trip of a lifetime! I was so excited and hooked on travelling, and I've been on travel adventures every year since.

It was a great combination, Pavlina and travel. Both have been amazing blessings in my life. We went on many epic trips around Europe and Australia. I liked the fact that she was exotic, open-minded, giving, easy-going, and open to trying new things. My compulsive drug-taking and excessive drinking stopped. She really was a calming influence in my life. Although I still had moments of depression and anxiety attacks, they were greatly reduced. I stayed with the health and fitness company until the beginning of 2003 when my differences with the assistant manager became unresolvable and she forced me to leave. The general manager made sure I received my base salary for the month. I went back to landscaping, working for another company, and we started saving for our planned four-and-a-half-month adventure, when we would lease a car and drive and camp all over Europe from May to October. This turned out to be another life-changing trip.

Some of the highlights of that trip included exploring Paris, visiting incredible castles, driving through the Pyrenees, visiting Alhambra in Spain, chilling out in Lisbon, kayaking in the north of Portugal, attending the Running of the Bulls festival in Pamplona, observing Snowflake the albino gorilla in the Barcelona Zoo, and seeing snow for the first time in Andorra. I will not forget being told to put my shirt on in the streets of Monte Carlo by a policeman, visiting the leaning tower of Pisa, or driving across Switzerland. Swimming in the lakes and hiking in the mountains was epic, as was exploring Budapest, the most underrated city in Europe. We experienced freezing in the ice caves of Slovakia, eating snails and then catching a hedgehog in Bratislava. The coast of Croatia is amazing with great seafood, diving, and quaint villages. And spending time in Prague is always fun. We went to Octoberfest for my birthday, and visited magnificent castles in Bavaria, spent a week in Ibiza, explored the canals of Venice, and had so many other amazing experiences.

Some of our first times together:

*First time ice skating at the Macquarie Centre in Sydney;

*Climbing the Sydney Harbour Bridge;

*Our first funeral, unfortunately her mother's funeral, after we spent three weeks with her;

*Many firsts in the bedroom and in nature;

*Exploring Europe on a four-and-a-half-month vacation;

*Eating sushi, our favourite food at the time;

*We stayed in our first castle together;

*And many first-time travel experiences mostly in Europe.

Pav, being older, was ready to settle down and start a family after our latest European adventure. I wanted to travel more, and I didn't feel ready to settle down. It was a challenging breakup, but it was the right thing to do. Although it was a clean break-up and we never saw each other again, I still missed her for years afterwards. Especially now looking back and reflecting, I know it was the right thing to do for my own personal growth and traveling kept depression at a distance. Mom still had contact with her before Pavlina's jealous husband banned her from seeing Mom only two years ago. Pav is living a couple of suburbs away from my mom and has two children, a boy and a girl. I'm happy she found happiness and is settled in Australia. As for me, I needed to follow my own path. Now I've been living in Bali for the last five and a half years. I haven't had a full winter since 2001, travelling to more than 50 countries across every continent except Antarctica. On average, every 60 days I'm in a different country, and I have no plans to ease up on my travels. I'm now involved in book publishing, personal development films, speaking, and I created this book series with the aim of sharing inspiring messages around the world.

Transformation can be as simple as doing something for the first time. For me, life is about experiences, finding my full potential, and helping other people to do the same. Travel is one of the best ways to experience and transform your life. It opens your mind to other cultures, and once the mind stretches, it will never be the same again. When was the last time you experienced something for the first time?

> "Nothing happens until the pain of remaining the same outweighs the pain of change."
>
> ~ Arthur Burt

CHAPTER TWO

The Running Man

By John Hanna
(with Timothy Marlowe)

A little boy is running through the streets, running for his life. The city is hot, full of noise and bright colours and odours both fragrant and foul, the yellow sun blazes from a deep blue sky high above the impossibly crowded streets below, and he *runs* through it all – the small face usually alive with glee and mischief now filled with something else. He knows this huge place like the back of his hand and weaves through the throngs with lightning speed, racing down narrow alleys, through bazaars, across squares lined with cafes where dark men sit drinking hot, sweet, black coffee, puffing on hookahs which envelop them in rich tobacco smoke, oblivious to the desperate figure that darts past and is gone.

Constantly looking back for signs of the pursuit, he jumps on and off trams and buses, his tiny body finding gaps in the crowd that no adult could possibly fit through, until finally his lungs give out and he collapses in a doorway:

panting, dripping with sweat, exhausted, but *safe*... for now.

That was 1967, the city was Cairo, and that little boy was me; I ran for my life then, and in one way or another it seems I've never *stopped* running. I was fleeing from my first and greatest adversary, and we'll return to him before the end to see if what came of it could possibly be worth the price. I've not spoken of this before, and I'm sharing it with you now because I finally feel ready, at age 55 and after a lifetime of fear and courage, to stop running.

I'm taking this opportunity to tell you my story in hopes of accomplishing three things: one, to entertain and inform and (maybe) even inspire you; two, to promote myself on the world stage (because in my heart I genuinely have a message that longs to find a voice); and three, to possibly heal myself of the demons that have pursued me for as long as I can remember, to bring that little boy peace, and (perhaps) allow the angels to take over now.

I know it's a lot to ask, but if we don't try we'll never know how much we're capable of. So I thank you in advance for taking the time to listen, and I'll do my best to make it worth your while, to not let you down.

ΔΔΔ

The title of this book, *Transformational Change*, describes life itself. We're all on a transformative journey full of riches and gifts at every step (if we could only see them), and we're constantly growing from lesser darkness to greater light. However, for most of us that's just a lovely fantasy, a fairy tale to give us hope along the way, and we don't truly *believe* it about our own reality.

The reason we don't believe is because so much that happens to us is challenging, or painful, or frightening, or just plain *hard*, and that simply doesn't fit our definition of either riches *or* light. My intention here is to give you courage by expanding your definition of positive and negative, of good and bad, until it encompasses *everything* that happens to you. Not just the happy and pleasurable things (which is easy), but the stuff we *don't* like and *don't* understand and wish had never happened (which is hard).

I swear to you on my children's lives that every person, thing, and event in the world has light and dark in equal measure, and when you truly get that absolutely *nothing* can stop you. For most people this takes a lifetime (if ever), but if I can help you begin to see this perfect balance in your own life, then my purpose will be achieved.

If you can find light in your darkness, victory in your defeats, clarity in confusion itself, you'll realise that you've always been *surrounded* by light, and your ultimate success is guaranteed. I hope that sharing my doubts and fears and blindness (and the gifts they concealed) will give you strength in the midst of your own journey, and you'll be encouraged to walk your path with a surer step and a lighter heart. It's only when we lose heart that we lose our way, and this is my story of how I learned to maintain my light in the midst of the darkness – and isn't that when we really *need* it?

'There are no obstacles on the path – obstacles are the path.'

~ Zen Proverb

So why am I so sure that every cloud has a silver lining, every negative an equal positive? It may sound strange coming from a man whose formal education isn't his strongest suit, but my certainty comes from, of all unlikely places... physics! This may get a little technical, but I'll make it very simple – and believe me, if *I* can understand it, so can you. I keep referring to light; physics says the entire universe is made up of matter and light, but that all matter is actually low-frequency, low energy, high density light. So believe it or not, it's *all* just light – and that means *everything*!

Now, how does light become matter? By splitting into positive and negative particles called positrons and electrons – they make up all matter, and they're always created in pairs. Every positron in the universe has a matching electron: they're called *complementary particles*, and are always exactly equal in power or *magnitude*.

You may be thinking right now, 'Okay, so what? What does any of that have to do with my life?' and the answer is – again, everything! Because this is no abstract science-y idea of test tubes and galaxies, it applies to everyone and every thing in the universe, and has profound implications.

What if you knew, with absolute certainty, that every dark or painful or challenging thing that ever happened (or *can* happen) to you has a guaranteed light and pleasurable and supportive side? Even further, physics says they must also be *instantaneous* – that is, they always appear together; so if every good and bad are equal, then the bigger the negative, the bigger the positive it comes with. That means the moment you have a little hassle, you simultaneously have a little help, somewhere, from some*one* or some*thing*. Likewise, a big problem automatically brings a big gift, and something life-threatening must also be... that's right, it has to be life-*giving*.

So, nice idea, right? Believe me, I know how far-fetched this sounds: we were never taught to think this way, and I don't expect you to accept it just because I say so; I know *I* wouldn't, so just file it away for now. But if it were true, wouldn't you have a different attitude to your journey of transformation– more confidence, more trust, more *courage* to face whatever the world brings you? Let's explore whether or not this 'fantasy' is true in my life, and as we go you may begin thinking about your own from a new perspective. I'll give you the dark side first, the world's view of such events, and then we'll come back to look for the light.

> **'When one door closes another door opens; but we so often look so long and so regretfully upon the closed door, that we do not see the ones which open for us.'**
>
> **~ Alexander Graham Bell**

I was born in Egypt in 1962, land of pharaohs and fakers, of great antiquity and even greater poverty. My family was deep in that poverty, so when I was seven we sailed off for a bright new life in a brand new country. But I wasn't happy about it; in fact (apart from the terror) I *loved* my home – big extended family, class captain, liked by all my teachers, total freedom and confidence to go anywhere – and on my first day in the new land I was punched in the face for riding a scooter I thought was free for all. Welcome to Australia, wog boy! God, I *hated* the place.

I didn't know where in the world we were: it was all so strange and alien, no one understood me and I couldn't understand them. All I could say was, 'Please. Yes. No. I'm sorry,' and not being able to communicate was both frustrating and frightening. Nobody talked or even *looked* like me: small and foreign and lost, I felt utterly worthless and alone – and as an added bonus, we were *still* poor.

Many years of grinding poverty followed: tiny flats in bad neighbourhoods, rats and cockroaches, hunger, my parents constantly worrying and arguing long into the night about money and even our *survival*. The details are in my book, but what stands out for me above all else is a deep and growing shame about being poor.

The last straw came at the age of 16, when my father gave me a dollar and told me to hop out of the car and get him a pack of cigarettes. When I got back he asked for his change, I said it was only 2¢ so I didn't bother, and he lashed out at me with such anger that I can still hear him forty years later; 'Do you know how *hard* I have to work for 2¢? Go get it!' When I went back into the shop with my tail between my legs the shopkeeper gave me a look of such bored contempt that I cringe to think of it even now. This was a turning-point for me, and I'll come back to it with the wisdom of hindsight.

So it was hard, but I survived my childhood, and when it came time for university my father decided my future. Money was crucial, so it was accountancy for me and off I went to become something I had absolutely no interest in. But no matter how hard I studied, my heart wasn't in it and I consistently failed every subject except law and economics – ironic and fateful, given my future.

I eventually dropped out, to my father's disbelief and horror, and took a lowly door-to-door sales job I loathed. I soon quit that as well, and then embarked on a long series of increasingly responsible but always unfulfilling sales and management positions: life insurance, savings bonds, savings and investment plans, and other equally tedious products. No matter what I sold, I realise now that I was actually trying to sell *myself* on the idea that I could get rich and be somebody, because deep down I feared I was no-one and nothing. Somehow during this time I acquired a wife and family, and my father died young and worn out, but wealth continued to elude me.

Those jobs were commission-only, so if I didn't sell we didn't eat. From sheer necessity I became quite skilful at the work I despised, and made great money for the time – $5,000 a week! This was so far beyond anything my father had ever imagined, and I felt like such a big man, that the inevitable happened and I got cocky. I stopped making sales, ran out of money, and pawned my father's ring (my only inheritance) to buy food. I planned to redeem it as soon as I 'got ahead', but I just kept going backwards; on the day I lost that last memory of him forever, it felt as though a part of me died with it. Eventually I couldn't afford the rent, so my wife and baby son moved in with her sister, I went back to live with my mother, and the old familiar shame became so overwhelming I could barely get out of bed in the morning.

Around this time I dragged myself to self-help business guru Robert Kiyosaki's seminar 'Money and You', and suddenly I no longer wanted to merely make money, now I wanted to touch and change the world! Oddly enough, at the very moment I made the decision to be of service to others, a colleague asked if I'd ever heard of something called 'negative gearing', and I was off to the races. The property company I created became a runaway success: we grew to fill multiple floors of an office building, and opened marketing, finance, and accounting wings. I eventually employed 40 finance brokers as well as 130 other staff, and became the largest Australian introducer of new business to Citibank.

The money absolutely *rolled* in, and I had everything I ever wanted: a beautiful big home, a loving wife and children, luxury cars, prestige, and success beyond my wildest dreams – so of course I sabotaged it all. I was wealthy, successful, respected… and still ashamed. You see, even though I'd achieved so much, I didn't feel I *deserved* it. I didn't understand taxation or reports or balance sheets, I just had a burning desire for wealth and knew how to motivate people, so I felt like a fraud;

unworthy of my achievements, and whatever we don't feel worthy of is taken (or given!) away.

So I was a national success, successfully hiding my secret fears, but it all came tumbling down the day my chief accountant said, 'John, we're ready to go international – I've set up a meeting with a top American firm, and their directors are flying in to set things up. This is the big time, baby!' He was excited, but I was devastated; I'd already been hiding from Australia, and now I'd have to hide from *America* too?

That was it for me, and I started running again – that weekend I began doing the things that only the most damaged and desperate people in our society turn to. I enthusiastically embarked on my new career of drug use and self-abuse, derailed the international expansion, and then set about destroying everything I'd spent so long creating. It wasn't easy, because the companies were so strong and my people so talented and loyal, but eventually I succeeded: over the next few years I lost the companies, the money, the cars and house, my family and friends, my self-respect, my health, and finally almost my life.

For a decade I drifted, quickly divesting myself of whatever money I still managed to scrape together, until four heart attacks finally got my attention. After 10 years to the month I at last decided enough was enough, stood up in my darkness and began to seek the light again. I was introduced to something called Universal Principles, the unseen laws of order and harmony which govern the apparent chaos of our lives, and *that* is what I want to share with you now.

I finally started taking personal responsibility for my world, really feeling the truth of the maxim, 'If it's to be, it's up to me,' and looking to see how those principles were playing out in the things that 'happened' to me. I've already shared the first of them with you – that everything in the world has two sides – and now I'd like to go back over the journey I've just described and see if it's true there. We'll explore it together, but remember that although we're talking about *me*, the real power lies in applying this principle to your *own* journey.

If you can't see the contribution that any person or event has made to you, you'll be resentful; you won't be grateful for them, or it, and *gratitude* is the key to greatness. Ingratitude for the gift of life harms only ourselves.

> **'Holding a grudge is like drinking poison and hoping someone else will die.'**
>
> **~ Spanish Proverb**

So, to sum up, the negative events I've described were: running in terror, leaving Egypt, inability to communicate, isolation, desperate poverty, university drop-out, drudgery, drugs, and the overwhelming shame that ran through it all. A pretty challenging mix, made up of many things the world labels 'bad', right? If I can find the light in this darkness, not just rationalisations but true *gifts*, would you be willing to allow that what I'm saying to you *might* be true? Okay, let's see – I'll go through them one by one, leaving the biggest and 'worst' for last.

I was unhappy about having to leave Egypt, but just look at what *came* of it. Would I want to be there now, with the heat, economic troubles, political instability, and war that country faces today? No way! I'd never have found the freedom and opportunities that came to me in my adopted country, and if I could speak to my younger self I'd take him by the hand, look into his eyes, and say, 'Wait! This is going to be a wonderful change for you, so don't worry. One day you'll be so grateful that it happened, I promise.' Thank god it *wasn't* up to me, because I'd have chosen familiar safety and lost all that was to come.

Being unable to speak the new language was frustrating, but today I'm bilingual and can speak to far more people around the world, which is what a public speaker craves, right? But not only that, the experience made communication so important for me that not only did I 'master' English but also learned how to communicate with body language, facial expression, humour, and pure good will, which has proved invaluable throughout my professional and personal life.

Being poor was a big one, and lasting as long and as intensely as it did (remember, every big negative must come with a positive of equal magnitude) meant there was a huge gift for me there. Scarcity is the cornerstone of desire, whatever is most missing in our lives becomes most important (a whole chapter of my book is dedicated to this vital concept), and it's at the core of a fundamental business principle – supply and demand. The less there is of something desirable the more valuable it is: the greater the scarcity the greater the hunger, and I was *starving*.

I was gifted with a deep, lifelong desire for great wealth, and creating it for myself and others has been a *major* focus for me. In fact, what I thought was the worst thing of all, the 2¢ humiliation, was actually the best thing that ever happened to me (and you can bet I'd have fought tooth and nail against *that* idea at the time). I went home and wrote a letter to my Uncle Wagdi, a highly-respected accountant, solemnly swearing that no matter *what* I'd become a millionaire, never being embarrassed or shamed about money like my father.

I said that was a turning-point; I didn't appreciate it at the time, but in that moment everything changed. Although the term didn't exist back then, that letter was my *mission statement* to myself, and I stayed true to it because the motivation was so powerful – I kept my word and became the wealthiest man in my family. But that moment set my destiny, and looking back I am profoundly grateful to the 'evil' shopkeeper – merely by curling his lip, he guaranteed my ultimate success. How efficient (and generous) a universe is *that*?

Next comes what I always thought of as the 'wasted' time spent at university. I didn't learn much from the classes, but it taught me an invaluable lesson – the importance of choosing my own destiny. That made me a leader not a follower, and those four years well-spent; I learned a great deal during that time, just not what I thought I was being taught, and that knowledge has saved me incalculable time on the journey to find myself – yet another brilliant 'mistake'.

I despised the sales work because I feared it was the culmination of my career potential, and that I'd be stuck there forever. I didn't realise it was merely an *apprenticeship*, and taught me so much: determination, sales technique, the ability to inspire others to work for me and themselves, and finally the ability to handle rejection and failure without becoming discouraged, which is absolutely *crucial* for a successful career, and life – because nobody wins all the time, and in truth our ability to handle defeat determines how high we can rise.

'Fall seven times, stand up eight.'

~ Samurai Proverb

Being alone felt terrible, but it taught me independence and self-determination, that no one would save me but *me* so I better stop waiting to be rescued, and one more thing. Friendship and loyalty have always been extremely important to me, they've helped me survive some very challenging times, and my companies are like one big family. It's something I rarely see in business, and has kept people loyal to me despite my many shortcomings.

So almost everything I judged at the time is now balanced: I found the gifts in the hardships, the light hidden in the darkness, and I wouldn't change a single thing because they made me who I am now, speaking to you from my heart about what life has taught this unwilling student. Have I kept my word to find true blessings in those events? For me, the answer is 'yes'.

That leaves three 'bads': drugs, shame, and running away– from the beginning and end of this story, and all intimately connected. I said I'd return to that little boy, and now's the time. I've never revealed this to anyone (or even *remembered* it except with a vague uneasiness) until the man who showed me Universal Principles helped me become aware of it and *all* its effects on me. Once I admitted the possibility to myself, the floodgates of memory opened and I remembered everything.

You see, I was fleeing my uncle, a man who'd repeatedly abused me sexually; I was too small to fight him, and too ashamed (again!) to tell anyone, so I ran for my life. The memory stayed buried all these years until I was ready to face it, but I believe it may have been *why* we left Egypt. If I'm grateful to live here rather than there, then I must also find a way to thank the circumstances that brought it about.

So at long last, with all my heart I'm able to say, 'Thank you!' for that childhood, and those experiences, and this life. How is that possible? This was my darkest event, but if my words have any truth in them it must also be the greatest source of light and transformation – so come with me one more time into the darkness to find it.

Believe me, it's no easy task – I know the magnitude of what I'm asking you to do. To succeed you must be absolutely honest not only about all the negatives, but also the *positives* that came with them, and that is difficult. Also, the more emotionally charged we are the harder it is to see clearly; someone else showed me the hidden blessings here, freeing me from self-judgment and shame, and I share it with you now in hopes it may lighten your own burden.

My friend came to me one day and said, 'John, I've been thinking about your uncle, why it happened, and what the gifts were.' 'Oh, really?' I said sceptically, because I couldn't find *anything* good about it, but was at least willing to listen. 'It was the earliest, worst thing ever, right?' '*Oh*, yeah!'

'So the key was to look for a link with your highest values. You have four qualities that made you so successful: an uncanny ability to read people, extraordinary charisma, powerful intuition, and huge anger – and they all came from *him*. You constantly act out that relationship, but make it work *for* instead of against you.'

I was quite shocked, and blurted, 'What?! What are you talking about?' because I immediately sensed he was right, although I had no idea how.

'You felt ashamed, that it was somehow your fault, right?'

'Yes, I did.'

'So you developed this ability to read people the moment you meet them, to protect yourself against ever being taken advantage of again, and don't you use that in business?'

'Every day.'

'You read people to keep yourself safe, then charm the hell out of them so they like you – to have power over them before they have it over you, as he did.'

I'd never thought of it that way before, but had to admit it was accurate.

'You didn't trust your rational mind anymore because it let this happen, so you developed a powerful intuition to tell you what your mind couldn't, and it's spookily accurate.'

I was getting overloaded now because the memories had started welling up, so I just nodded dazedly.

'And finally, anger. You use it to overpower people, or for the energy to meet challenges – you *use* your anger as a tool. It all fits: reading and charming to be *safe*, intuition to *know*, and anger to *arm* you against it ever happening again. Your life is a direct result of that little boy being pushed to grow in extraordinary ways.

'That event was the seed of your greatness, but because you didn't understand *why* it happened you split yourself up over it, and the shame sabotaged what it didn't feel worthy of. That's why you've made and lost so much, so often – understand and embrace *both* sides of what happened, and you'll get to keep it all.'

It all rang true. Now I simply couldn't speak, and just looked at him with tears in my eyes – tears not of pain or sadness, but understanding. Those qualities were the foundation of all my achievements – true gifts, and the direct result of what had seemed pure evil.

Every great business leader I've ever met (in fact every great *person*) relied on a powerful intuitive sense. They may not have called it that – a lot of men in particular will have a 'gut feeling', or say that 'something didn't smell right', but they're just describing in sensory terms something that comes from a higher part of us, and transcends the physical. Intuition is above the senses, higher than instinct, and beyond the conscious mind – intuition is a mysterious, holistic knowing, with absolute certainty, something that our rational mind cannot explain.

I can't tell you how many times my intuition has stepped in and told me not to hire someone, or go into a partnership, or take a risky (but *so* attractive) step in my career, to do or not do something, and that guidance later proved not only accurate but *invaluable*. I didn't always listen, particularly when my emotions were involved, but through painful experience I've learned to ignore my intuition at my peril. Time and again, the people and things I was warned about later proved to be unreliable, or dishonest, or destructive, and listening to that inner voice has saved me millions of dollars and even more precious years of time.

From seeming powerlessness and poverty of spirit came all I have now, and when I finally saw the truth I was speechless with gratitude. Now, I'm not saying I'm wise enough yet to actually be able to *thank* my uncle, and I certainly wouldn't presume to dictate how anyone else treated this way should deal with it, but if those events were the price I paid for a lifetime of wealth and freedom and opportunity, then I'd have to say that, for *me*, it was a good deal. From that terrible event have come great gifts, and that's true for all of us: the greater the darkness, the greater the light it calls forth, and the more power of transformation.

The shame of feeling *less* than I thought I should be has been an incredible spur to be *more* than I thought I *could* be; it shielded me from complacency and kept me going when so many others have fallen by the wayside, or simply stopped growing. I must be extraordinary just to *feel* ordinary, so strangely enough I do much more thanks to my shame than I'd ever have done without it.

And drugs? Well, on one level they were simply the most efficient way to get rid of everything I thought I didn't deserve, and they did it incredibly well. They also helped me feel (at least temporarily) powerful when I felt so powerless – *nobody* does anything without a pay-off, a pleasure, and that was mine. But most importantly, when I was in the depths of my darkness I met Tim Marlowe, who helped me find the light there. Not only that, he had the insights about my uncle that made sense of everything for me, and is now my dearest (and as he says, 'most unlikely') friend and co-writer. He appeared as a direct result of the drugs, and for that alone I can thank them wholeheartedly – again, the gift was worth the price.

∆∆∆

So, would you agree that I've found the hidden blessings in those difficulties, a light in the darkness that is of equal magnitude? But that's for me – now how about *you*? We always have a choice between reaction and action, ignorance and wisdom, dark and light, and all we really have to do is *choose*; it's at one time the simplest and hardest of all choices. But if it were easy, everyone would do it, right? It's really not for the masses – that's why it's called *mastery*!

Mother Theresa once said, 'I know God would never give me any more than I can handle, I just wish he didn't trust me so much.' And it's the same for all of us: we're never given more than we can handle, so if you've had a lot of hard darkness there must be an equal amount of strong light within you – encouraging, yes? But being *able* to do something doesn't necessarily mean that we *will*: we're all *able* to eat or doubt or fear less, able to exercise or love or be grateful more, but we don't always *do* it – so this may help.

I've said everything is light, and that it's all balanced, yes? Light splits into perfectly balanced positrons and electrons, and human *consciousness* splits into perfectly balanced positive and negative *emotions*. Both sides have only half the power, and when reunited their true nature is revealed – particles become light in the world of physics, and emotions become love and wisdom in the world of human beings.

This is easy enough to understand theoretically, but much more difficult to apply in reality. It's hard to learn to swim when you're drowning, so start with something easier than the often-scary present – your own past. Choose a 'negative' event in your life and start listing all the positive results that flowed from it, and don't stop until the positives exactly equal the negatives. Look into all seven areas of life: spiritual, mental, vocational, financial, family, social, and physical; and the entire time line from then 'til now. You'll know you're done when you can honestly say, 'Thank God that happened, I wouldn't change a thing!'

That, my friends, is how to 'magically' transform emotions into love and wisdom, and it's a power known to all true masters; in fact, it's the *essence* of mastery. Balancing your perceptions of good and bad takes you out of your fearful mind and into your courageous *heart*, where nothing happens that you can't handle – and here's why it works.

Every time I got cocky or above myself, something would always humble me and put me in my true place. Likewise, every time I lost heart and felt *less* than I truly was, something or someone would appear to help me and lift me back up, into the centre where our true power dwells. That's why this principle is so profound and effective, because life *itself* is using it to help us become who we're meant to be.

So we can relax and trust the world to do that for us, but the thing is it's quite *slow*. It takes time for these forces to play out, swinging wildly from false highs to false lows as we imagine we're winning or losing – and both are half-truths. Stay true to yourself: don't buy into temporary illusions of triumph and disaster, and you'll rise much faster. The more you can see everything that happens to you as *on* your way rather than *in* your way, the stronger and more certain you will be, and the less you'll fear anything. Use your mind to equilibrate *yourself* and the universe won't have to do it, slowly and often painfully, for (or *to*) you.

Freeing yourself from elation and depression about the half-truths awakens you to the whole truth – that *everything* is a gift – and you regain your whole self, and the ability to manifest the life you'd love. It's not easy (nothing truly worthwhile ever is), but hopefully these words will provide the light to master any darkness you may encounter.

We're almost done now – there's only a little more I have to share, and it's at the core of my message to you.

'The will of God is equilibrium.'

~ St. Augustine, Christian Mystic

And he was absolutely right. St. Augustine used the word 'God', but whatever that means to you – Spirit, the Creator, the Universe itself – it's true, and is our last Universal Principle. All things seek balance, and the more you equilibrate your mind and emotions the closer you approach that balance point, the centre. And as with all things: atoms, solar systems, galaxies… and humans, the *centre* is where the power lies.

And what is at the centre of human beings? The *heart*. In my life, everything I put my heart into flourished and grew, and everything I tried to do without it, or lost heart about, withered and died. The First Nations People of North America taught their children to find 'the path with heart', and it's as true today as it was long ago.

Come to the centre, and everything changes; that's where your heart is, your love and wisdom and gratitude for life. Gratitude for what is, *exactly* as it is, gives you great power to direct and determine what will be. Heartfelt thanks for your past will give you a future you can be grateful for, and without your having to actually change *anything*, you'll be utterly transformed.

Now, don't mistake me on this – challenge and difficulty are real and powerful forces; good and bad do exist in our perceptions until we develop the wisdom to see their true nature, and they occur in every aspect of life. But here's the point: if you're going to get lessons and guidance in the form of positive and negative experiences no matter *what* you do, you might as well get them in the pursuit of what you love rather than what you don't, doing what inspires you, not what just tires you. I'm not suggesting the pain and pleasure will end – far from it; in fact they'll actually *grow* in magnitude along with your potential, but they'll be *worth* it, and you'll be bigger to handle them.

'You are never given a dream or inspiration without also being given the power to make it real, but you may have to work for it.'

~Richard Bach, author of
Jonathan Livingstone Seagull

Don't let your fearful mind sabotage your inspired dreams; you were given them for a reason and they won't be denied. Although my brain isn't my strongest suit, I've been smart enough to not let it run my life and relied instead on the part of me that *knows* – my heart. I've always wanted to be a writer, even though 'logically' it was absurd as I'm barely literate. But because I never let go of that dream, it drew in someone whose gift turns my thoughts into works of art – if you can *see* it, you will *be* it.

He's a great writer and counsellor, but has no business sense whatsoever; he simply doesn't care about it, but in the things he loves – language and literature and knowledge – he's an absolute genius, and I believe we're all the same. Whatever we truly love, we have a spark of genius about, and it's up to each of us to find that genius, and then give it all we have – to fan that spark into a living flame, and it will turn transform us in ways we can't presently imagine.

There's a single word that sums up what we love ('the path with heart'), and that word is *purpose*. I haven't time to do more than introduce it here, but it's why you were put on this Earth; most people never discover it and spend their lives on lesser tasks devoid of inspiration, so true fulfillment escapes them. I've co-authored a book with Tim that focuses on how to find this crucial element, bringing your whole mind and heart to some inspired purpose and using it to create a magnificent life – if this story somehow spoke to you, you'll love *The Way of the Wealthy* (on Amazon).

So here we are at the end of our long journey together, coming full circle back to what I believe is at the centre of everything – the human heart. Just before he died my father wrote me a letter I've cherished, calling me by an Egyptian word which means 'he who follows his heart'. He was a simple man, but he had clear sight. I've always tried to live by that principle, and I realise now that his ring wasn't my true inheritance, it was this inner quality which cannot be pawned, or lost, and will never leave me. The truth is always with us, and it has finally allowed me to stop running.

I hope you've enjoyed reading this as much as I did writing it, but all good (and bad) things must come to an end, and our time is up for now. Before I go I'd like to share one more spark of ancient wisdom whose beautiful words have given me confidence when I felt I'd lost my way, and are my last gift to you; may they be a light in your darkness, and a reminder that all troubles pass.

'It is said that all things will be well in the end, so if all is not well, it must not yet be the end.'

~ Hindu Scripture

Trust this, and never give up. Time and wisdom will reveal the blessings of your life, as they have for me; my greatest challenges were my greatest gifts, and so are yours. Realise that simply by changing your *mind* you can transform your entire world, and that is true magic. The most miraculous transformation occurs daily, yet we take it for granted – the dawn of a new day.

No matter how long the night, the sun always rises, and so will you.

"Transformation itself isn't a joy.

The joy is in the freedom that arrives

just past the threshold. It rushes through.

Released like rain."

~ Victoria Erickson

CHAPTER THREE

Dare to Redefine Yourself

By JoJo Bennington

re: defined - *meaning:* re-examined for the purpose of change

When I first was given the opportunity to be a part of this collaboration, I was so excited! I think I wrote this chapter in record time. But then, I went into self doubt, what do I have to offer? What do I have to say? Who am I to tell my story? Who cares? So I sat on it, nervous to send back my edits, sick to my stomach. But then, I realized I was making it about me, and not the people it may help. If even one person sees themselves in this story and can move forward from a painful place, then that's all that matters. The self doubt can be stifling at times, but I will feel the fear, silence the noise in my head, breathe, and step through. Ok, let's go..)

Not What I Had Planned

18 years old, sitting in the holding cell of the jail, arrested on drug and possession charges, was not how I thought I

would enter into adulthood. I remember that hard bench, the smells, the cries, the women who were sharing this square box with me who were so obviously broken in some way. I couldn't help but look at them and wonder 'how broken was I'? I found myself addicted to crack cocaine, selling my jewelry and my soul, stealing money, lying, cheating, and doing things so out of character for who I thought I was; remembering, that just the night before, I was sitting on the floor of a house that I can only describe as a slum, getting high with a woman who was eight months pregnant. I physically shuttered. Not from the cold cell, concrete floors and wooden bench, but from the disgust in myself. How can this be me? Is this my life? Who had I become? Who had I followed down this rabbit hole? What the hell was I thinking? I went through the humiliating experience of calling my parents to bail me out, begging anyone who would listen that this was not my life, and having to endure the most degrading experience of the cavity search by the guards. Bend over, spread em', cough. Oh yeah, that's how it's done while you are naked and scared. Seriously, this was not what I had planned. The bruises on my arms and neck that had been placed there by my drug-addicted, abusive, unfaithful, rapist boyfriend were not even the worst of the marks that I had been allowing myself to endure. Right then and there, I made the decision that this was not to be my future.

Growing up in Las Vegas, I had had so many dreams when I was a kid: actor, dancer, comedian, choreographer, astronaut, princess... queen of the world. I was always told that I could be whatever I wanted. Where did I go wrong? Did I need a man so badly that I would follow him to hell? Apparently I needed something that he was giving, but I decided I didn't want it anymore. The belt marks across my ass that have left a permanent scar on my skin and mind, reminded me that this man who had said he loved me was clearly expressing this "love" in a very non-loving way. This was how I was reminded to stay in line, or maybe just that he had had a bad day.

When my mother picked me up from jail, I slumped into the car feeling ashamed, and I told her everything that had been happening (well, almost everything). I had made the decision that I would never do drugs again. I went home and went through the mind-blowing effects of detoxing off of crack without professional help. It wasn't so much the physical pain, but the mental anguish that was even worse. The horrible, evil dreams every night (several times, I truly think I was being tempted by the actual devil itself), the constant nagging in my head to get high, the pull to go be with people who were not good for my new life...it was so difficult, but I just took it moment by moment, day by day, and I did it. I never used crack or cocaine again.

I remember there was a commercial on TV that was supposed to talk you *out* of getting high. It elaborately showed a glass pipe with this colored smoke swirling around it, and little crack rocks sitting next to it. It was mesmerizing. Every time it came on TV, I could actually SMELL it. Once the commercial was over I WANTED to go get high; obviously, not the effect they were going for. They did finally take it off TV after I explained to the organization that they were not helping addicts stay sober, nor were they convincing anyone to quit, instead it was quite the opposite. It's funny that over 30 years later, I can still identify the smell in a crowd. The smell always reminds me, the hold will forever be with me.

But, I had done it. I had freed myself.

I was a fighter.

I was redefining myself before I even knew what that meant.

Even going back to that man who was so bad for me, because I hoped I could save him as well, just made me stronger, made me tougher, made me self-sufficient, made me independent, made me brutally honest. So much so, that people on the outside just saw the tough exterior.

That bad guy was not my first mistake when it came to men. I repeated that pattern, not with the drugs, but with the abuse. I went through another relationship where I was physically, mentally, and emotionally hurt. At the end of that relationship my definition of myself was again challenged. Even though I had endured such pain, and tried so hard to make it work, I was unfaithful in the end...always looking for something that I wasn't getting. From that time forward, truth, loyalty and faithfulness became a part of my being as much as breathing. It was so hard for me to be the reason that the relationship ended. I had endured so much, how could it be my fault? It wasn't fair.

It wasn't until much later that I was taught how to take 100% of the responsibility for every situation, whether it was my fault or not. Fault didn't matter, blame didn't matter. Only putting a clean end to a situation mattered, then there was nothing left to fester. "Oops sorry, my bad." Whether or not it was...that lesson that was still years away.

After that ordeal ended, I was a little tougher, a little more guarded. But I still believed in people. I thrived off of my friendships with others. I gave everyone the benefit of the doubt. I believed that everyone had good in them, even the people who had hurt me so much, because I knew that I was a good person at heart, and if I could do such bad things, then other people could be the same. Even though I was defined as tough, I was very soft at the heart of it. A giver. A planner. All-inclusive. People just had to get closer to me to find that out.

Never Say Never

I remember saying as a teenager, just because I grew up in Vegas, does not mean I will be a black jack dealer. (To be honest, I remember saying I wouldn't do a lot of things that I ended up doing, like being addicted to drugs and letting someone hit me.) So when I went to apply for a front desk management job at the new MGM hotel, and they said "We love your personality, we have a better offer for you...we will teach you how to deal blackjack, which will be way more lucrative for you"; and that's how, eight weeks later, I found myself auditioning for the position of blackjack dealer at the fanciest new casino on the strip. And for almost the next 10 years, I worked from 9pm to 5am, dealing cards, handling drunk people, breathing in tons of cigarette smoke, and understanding for the first time what it could do for my life to make a good living wage. I wasn't rich, but I was very comfortable. Dealing also helped me develop my biting, quick wit and personality a bit more, and it was fun! At least it was for about the first year. After that, it began to feel mundane. It made me feel crazy to count to 21 every night, thousands of times. It felt like a dead end. Again, I had done something I said I would never do, and again found myself unhappy with my decision. I just knew there was something else out there for me. I didn't like myself very much. I felt a sense of being lost. It was as if I could look down at my chest and see a gaping hole there. I didn't feel inspired, and even worse, I didn't inspire anyone else either. What was my purpose? I wanted something of my own.

The New Guy

Out with friends one night at a bar in Vegas, I met a guy. Yeah, you know the story...our eyes met from across the room, and we were instantly attracted to each other. That guy, Vinnie, was a former marine, current electrician, who was over six feet tall. (I always asked the height first, as my mother had put a height requirement on my next guy of at least 5'10", because all of my former abusers had been short. My dad was also short, but that's a whole deep dive into some other part of my psyche that is not for this story.) Vinnie was handsome, had amazing blue eyes, could dance and sing, and was a ton of fun. Within a short time, we were engaged. He didn't hit or hurt. We could argue with just words. Two years after we met, we were married. Things felt good, but deep down inside, I felt like I wanted more. Having a good man in my life was great, but it wasn't enough to fill up that gaping hole. It helped, but, I knew there was something out there for me. What was it? What could it be?

TANtalizing

One night at the casino, this guy sat down at my table - a friendly man who owned tanning salons in Arizona. He was in town for a convention about the tanning industry. I was intrigued. I had used a tanning bed myself, loved to have a tan, and as the night went on, the thought of having my own salon began to feel exciting. I picked his brain for hours, and at the end of the night he offered me his two passes to the convention for the following day. That was in July. By January, my sister Sherry and I had opened a salon in a new shopping center in an emerging part of town. TANtalizing tanning salon was born, and it was an immediate hit.(Name credit goes to Vinnie). We felt strongly about teaching people to tan a safe way, and bring more education. I quit my job at the casino, we opened a second salon, and then a third location. It was hard work, long hours, but I loved it. We did it all, from sales, to cleaning, to changing lamps in the beds, to laundry, to payroll. It was rewarding. It was my baby. What it wasn't, was freedom.

Sometimes we think, 'when I have my own business and no one else to answer to, then I will be free.' But instead, what had to be done was a daily grind to be there, to put the key in the door every single day, or we didn't make money. We didn't have the freedom to come and go as we pleased. We had to be there to cover shifts and make sure things were in order every day. It's also tough to be in business with family. No matter how much I loved my sister and she loved me, our family dynamic was brought into this space and we fought - not a lot - but enough. We did things differently. We saw things differently. It was all a learning experience, but emotionally it was tough on all of us. My husband didn't always see things eye to eye with my sister either, and that became difficult, as I was constantly in the middle; me defending her to him, or me defending him to her. It started to weigh on me. There were a few moments when I wondered if both the business and the marriage would fail. I began to feel that longing again...that there was something more for me. Was this what I really wanted long term? And yes we had a business, but we were not flourishing. Maybe it was time for my sister and I to just be sisters again. After six years, I started to think of selling.

But, who was I? What did I know? Where would I go? What would I do? What did I have to offer? I wanted to inspire. To help. To do something of value in the world. I wondered what I had actually contributed to the world. I felt like it had been nothing of any value. Deep down, I felt a bit like a failure. I was a recovered drug addict, who tanned people for a living, could count to 21, and most people who didn't know me, saw me as mean and unapproachable. Great place to start from... (Yeah that was said with a sarcastic flair, one of my specialties.) But I did have passion. I had drive. I was a worker. I could do whatever I put my mind to. I was a good person who desired to do good things. My intuition told me there was something out there for me that would really light me up. I had learned to trust my gut enough to pay attention. I had not yet fully defined who I was, and all of those things were me, the good and the bad, but they didn't define me completely. There were so many more blank spaces to fill in. I knew I hadn't tapped my potential yet.

Defining Health

What did fire me up a bit was health. I had taken up an interest in nutrition after a naturopath had helped me with my own health. Maybe I could go back to school, become a nutritionist, open a practice, and help people regain their health. My husband had a good job, maybe he could help me go back to school and start again.

Do you ever notice that when you start to think of something, when you begin to search, the right people and situations just seem to show up? Well, that's definitely what happened for me again. I was searching for nutrition schools and I was also looking to add to my health regimen. I had healed my painful stomach a lot from my work with my naturopath, but still wasn't back to 100%. That's when this guy showed up in my face at a health and wellness expo and asked me if I had ever cleansed. Well yeah, I had, I was in the middle of one right then! I was miserable, felt awful, and said I would never cleanse again. I told him to go away, I even physically made the sign of the cross at him with my fingers like he was vampire. But my sister was there with me, and she listened to him. She signed up for some cleanse products and said she wanted to bring them into the tanning salon to sell. I said, "Do what ya want, but don't tell me anything about it!"

Haha, there was my pattern again! 'I will NEVER do that.' Always pushing my NEVER button over and over again. I watched my sister go through this cleansing system and she did amazing, looked great, even her skin was glowing. So I said, "OK get me the stuff...but I don't want to hear one thing about selling this crap!" I got some products for myself and for Vinnie so we could do it together. And we did. And all I can say is, I shifted. My body, my mind, my focus, my skin, my energy, my sleep, my cravings, heck even colors looked brighter and sharper. If this is what it means to feel good, then I had never felt good my whole life. Vinnie had the same experience. My friends, the same. People from the salon, the same. For Real? What's in this stuff?

One morning waking up, still in twilight sleep, I thought to myself, 'I have helped so many people with this system, I am doing the exact thing I wanted to do, which was help people get healthy and regain their quality of life'. Why go back to school for four years to open a practice and start from scratch? Why couldn't I just sell this stuff? Could I sell enough to make a difference? I started to do some research. Over the past few years, I had become a research nut, so I put my research skills to work and investigated every ingredient, every herb, processing and packaging practice, efficacy testing practices, the company founder, the co-founders, and the formulator of this system. It took me a diligent two weeks worth of time to check out a mere seven products. At the end of this two weeks, I was in. I was sold. I had 'drunk the juice'. I had never done research before where the deeper I looked the better it got. Usually, it was the opposite. I told Vinnie I wanted to sell the tanning salons and do this nutrition thing full time. He thought I was crazy, but he also supported my choice. In the back of my mind, I had also hoped it would help our troubled relationship around the salon subject.

To give me confirmation that I was on the right track, I put the salons up for sale on some obscure business opportunity site, and two days later, a cute little blonde, be-bopped through the door with her agent looking for a business to buy. About 45 days later, we were out, money in hand, all three salons no longer ours. It was bittersweet for sure. I was excited, scared, and ready for the next chapter of my life.

SHHH.. Listen, Here's The Secret

I had no idea what was about to happen to my life. To my heart. To my mindset. To my view of the world. Once I jumped in to meet my new endeavor head on, I realized that I was now involved in the network marketing industry, and how proud I was of this company that was doing it all 'the right way'. I decided to go to a company event to learn more. After the event, one of the leaders in the company, Lenny, asked me if I would stay to watch a new video that was out. He said the video would change the way I thought, and perhaps even my life. I trusted him and stayed to watch. That night in a dark conference room, surrounded by others in our company, I was introduced to *The Secret*. The book and video created by Rhonda Byrne brought the conversation about the Law of Attraction to a public forum. I cried, I smiled, I was shocked. I came to realize that I had been the creator of ALL of the things that had taken place in my life. The good, the bad, the very bad. The hurt, the pain, the dismay, the happy, the joyful and also the peace; I was responsible for it all. Throughout my life, I had believed that life was just happening to me. It was just in my cards to be hurt, let down, or broken hearted. The world was just unfair. Some people were just lucky, but that wasn't me. It was while watching this video that I realized how important the power of choice really was. I learned that in every second, I had the power to choose. I could choose my thoughts now, my responses, my intentions, my focus, and all that was created would appear in my life. It was all ME. Just as it is all YOU. I believed it from the first moment I heard it. There was no doubt about it, I was in charge. We are all in charge and have access to this blueprint. And so began my love of what we know as personal growth. My love of intention and thoughts, belief, vision, and the magnificent power of our own internal words grew quickly. I wasn't a pro at it. I played ping pong in my head constantly, positive thoughts battling negative thoughts. But as each thought came and went, I got better at controlling them. It was daily work and I didn't always win.

Who Cares, I Quit

I had been living this life of service to others' health. Over time, I had coached hundreds of people and had built a small team who had the same passion. I was making a small, decent income. I was working on my mindset, vision and goals. Things were moving along nicely, not quick, but progressing forward. Then along came this girl who was new to the company, with a passion and influence that was amazing, and she blew by me as if I was standing still. She was moving through the company ranks faster than me and earning more income too. I was happy for her, but I soon began to compare myself to her, which is the worst thing we can do. It will never be a fair match. I knew that, others told me that, but I couldn't help but feel 'less-than'. How many times had I heard the phrase "Comparison is the thief of joy"? Then on top of this comparison struggle, I had a couple of new clients who were complaining about how they were feeling. They didn't understand what it takes to rebalance a body. I let it all weigh on me. I was sad and irritated, never a good space to create a beautiful life from. I decided that this health business just wasn't for me...that I couldn't do it. Plus, I was battling Vinnie everyday because he hated network marketing. So I told my mentor George Ruiz, I said flat out, "I Quit." I told him how I felt, how worn down I was. I knew my mindset was in the wrong place, but I couldn't manage to get hold of it. It was too much. I was done. This happened when I was just passing my two-year mark. George told me, "JoJo, you have no idea what you can create here, or the possibility that is out there for you. What I know is, you can do this. I believe in you. And until *you* can believe in you, borrow *my* belief in you. I commit to work with you and help you through this. Vinnie will come around... eventually. I believe in you".

No one had ever said things like this to me before. I didn't want to be a quitter. Quite the contrary, I wanted to finish this one out and see the results, so I decided to stay and got to work. I shifted my mindset. I tried to ignore Vinnie's negativity and unconscious sabotage. I began to understand that his behavior was just his way of coping as well.

Sometimes we just need someone to give us a pep talk, to believe in us and to lift us up. I still search out those people in my tough times, and I hope that you have people in your life that can be that rock for you. If not, seek them out. They are our angels.

I did decide to go on to become certified in Nutrition and Wellness. It helped boost my credibility and knowledge, and it also increased my ability to help others, which I had really found was my greatest passion: to help, to teach, to share my knowledge, and to continue learning to repeat this positive cycle over and over again. This had become my new drive. When I was actually inspiring and supporting others, I felt like I was contributing to the world.

Everything was in flow - well, everything except how Vinnie felt about what I was doing for a living. He "said" he supported me, but he really didn't. I did my nutrition thing, he did his electrician thing, and we tried not to talk about my thing too much. Then it happened. The economy tanked. Everyone thinks that gaming is the biggest industry in Las Vegas. It's not. The biggest industry is construction. Everything is always being newly modeled or remodeled on a perpetual basis. Then we woke up to 2008, and the majority of the working construction laborers were sent home with no job and no vision of a job in sight. Many were on unemployment for the first time. It lasted several long years. They lost health insurance. They lost the ability to support their families. And they lost the feeling that they were the men and women that they once thought they were. They were defining themselves by their J.O.B. Many gained weight, became depressed, and lost hope. I watched all of this happen to my big, strong guy. He sat day after day on the couch, watching the news, playing angry birds and arguing politics on Facebook. As you can imagine, this was a very negative space to be in.

It was a very difficult time in our marriage. I invited him to come work with me, but he would just repeat, "nope, not for me, that's your thing". I knew I had to get moving if I was going to make up for his lost income, so that's what I did. I always had it in me to build an incredible team, and that's who began to show up, incredible people! Over the next two years, while he sunk further into depression, I paid off all of our bills, our cars, and our credit cards. The only thing outstanding was a very manageable mortgage payment. I never told him I did it. I never told him that I had quietly tripled his weekly income. Never, until one day. He was staring at the computer, looking at the calls from the union hall, and he said in a defeated tone, "There are just no calls, I am never going back to work". I couldn't hold it in any longer. I told him that he didn't ever have to go back if he didn't want to - that I had increased our income and paid off all of our bills. He didn't get it. He stared blankly at me trying to comprehend what I had just said. I even had to show him our zero balance credit card statements and both of our car titles that had been paid off. He asked, "When did you do this?" I told him I had done it while he had been sitting there, becoming the angry birds champion of the world and feeling sorry for his situation. Seeing another opportunity to invite him to come work with me, I offered up the proposal, and believe it or not, even after all I had just said to him, he said, "Nope", once again.

The Shift

Luckily during Vinnie's time of depression, I had amazing mentors around me. Remember Dave, that guy I had made the sign of the cross at so many years ago when he asked if I had cleansed? Well, he had become my powerful mindset mentor. I was also blessed with the friendship of his wife Cary, who stood by me and supported me in my hardest and darkest moments of self doubt. And then there is David Wood, who is one of the brightest lights in my world.. He's always totally honest with me, always approaches me with love, although sometimes a little tough. He's taught me what life can truly be like and how to live every moment to the fullest. If I didn't have enough stories to tell, I had to get out and have experiences. One of the biggest things that he did for me was to tell me that I deserved a spouse who truly supported me and wanted to live life to the fullest and that I must also do the same. He asked me to bring Vinnie along to a retreat on his island in Belize for a training. I invited Vinnie to come. He resisted. But, he realized, that if I continued to grow and he did not, that eventually we would grow apart. He agreed that he didn't know what he didn't know (a good lesson for us all), and he came. Though he struggled, spending that week with David and a whole island of network marketers, the experience helped to shift his perspectives of himself, my chosen profession, and essentially the world. We came home with a new vision to work toward together, to create amazing things. It was such a relief for me. I knew in my heart as we were leaving to go to the island, that we were either leaving together with a new outlook, or we were leaving apart to embark on separate lives. Coming home, I could take a breath knowing we were going to work things out. Thank goodness for David. I am grateful that today, he is still there to help me through my toughest moments.

Who Wants To Be A Millionaire?

Someone told me when I started this network marketing profession that I would be a millionaire in this company. I agreed, "Heck yeah I will!" But I really had no concept of what that meant. Finally achieving this status in our company was an incredible moment. The owners of the company called us during their trip to Singapore to congratulate us on becoming the company's 164th Millionaires. We were invited to tell our story on stage at the next big event. We were given perks and listed in the company's top list. All of these things were 'outside accolades', but what it really gave me, was a deep knowing that I wasn't a failure. It gave me a feeling of satisfaction for accomplishing such a goal, and a deep sense of pride and gratitude for the incredible team of people that we had helped to build, who were the backbone of everything. I was deeply grateful for George, who had talked me out of leaving many years before, because if I had, I would have never known what this was like. I couldn't even imagine it back then. I thought I could, but not really.

Do you know what the most amazing thing was? As Vinnie and I were invited to stage to tell our story, I said my thank you's and a few words about persistence, and I handed the microphone to Vinnie. In a choked up voice, he said to the room of 8,000 people, "Guys out there, don't be like me. Don't secretly hope that your wife will fail just so you can be right. Support them 100% and you can be up here too." The audience choked up with him, felt his heart, and agreed they would not be that guy in their women's lives. What that moment was for me was a realization that I wasn't crazy. What I had felt all those years, had really been true. And to hear him admit it, and to understand how scary that must have been for him, well, it was an incredible moment. I experienced a feeling of success that I had never known before. It was a feeling of love for him that was all-encompassing. It also reminded me of how many women had probably felt the same way that I had: defeated, less than, just getting through every day, and giving up on their dreams. A new spark was ignited within me.

Redefining Women

I love helping people get their health and vitality back. It fires me up! But going through all I had gone through in my life, taking my life back from drugs, abuse, and a serious lack of self-worth, has helped me see that my deepest passion truly lies in empowering women. Not in a 'dominance over men' way, but in a way that allows them to stand in their own feminine power...to see, feel and fully embrace their own worth. So often, women lose themselves to things like lack of self-esteem, or lack of self-belief. There are people who expect women to only be mothers, or wives, or some other label that doesn't truly define their unique individuality. We, as women, can lose our voices. We become angry and frustrated. We lose the ability or reasoning to forgive. We lose the loving, feminine hearts that are truly unique to the woman.

These are just a few of the reasons that I have co-founded the UP Retreats (Unlimited Potential) with my nutrition partner and friend Cary. She too helps women find their true inner voice. My journey to be able to find my beauty, my worth, and my heart, and to be able to truly forgive those that I have felt hurt by is my newest journey, my biggest path and hopefully a welcome contribution to the world. Redefining myself as a women's empowerment coach has given me the most joy of all, so far. To see someone who is feeling so low, so broken and to be able to help them look in the mirror and see themselves, maybe for the first time...to see the light bulbs go on and the smiles begin to come back, has been one of my most rewarding moments in life.

We are all beautiful beings. We all have worth in this world. We all have a purpose. It is my wish to help our souls see it in ourselves.

Dare To Redefine You

How could this silly teenager with a drug problem, who may have ended up in jail with a ruined life, this woman who allowed herself to stay and be beaten down, raped, and diminished, come back to rise up and contribute to the world in a way that lights her up?

I **CHOSE** it. I chose to redefine who I was in the world. I was not born any of *those* things, I had created them. I was not born broken. I was born perfect, just as you were. And I learned that I could create anything I wanted to be. Just as Vinnie wasn't born an electrician, or a marine, he could learn to redefine his perception of himself and transform into whatever he **CHOSE**. This is not a unique power. This is an inherent power that we are all born with.

In the book *A Happy Pocket Full of Money,* David Cameron Gikandi writes, "You can intend and create into the past, just as effectively as you normally intend into the future." This passage baffled me, because how can we go back and re-create something in the past that has already happened? It's already over, how do we fix that? Then it hit me: it's the gift in the lessons of life. It's thinking back to reverse engineer the situation, or event, or hurt, to find the thing that you are so grateful for now. As a small example, I am so grateful for my drug problems, as they have shown me how strong I really am and how I do NOT want to live my life. Sometimes it is hard to see the gift, but it's always there. Understanding this has taught me forgiveness in a way I hadn't known before, and it has allowed me to look at my "offenders" with new eyes. It has allowed me to forgive myself. That little sentence has shifted my whole thought process, and is so much a part of my 'WHY' for wanting to teach people how to move through anger and hurt in order to forgive. It will be my next journey of redefinition.

I share my story, not so you can feel sorry for my path or any of my pain, but so you may find hope in the struggle. Become aware of your patterns by hearing about mine. Love your lows, for they have led to your highs. Look back and be grateful for whatever situation you may have been feeling bad for and give it a new definition. Know that you own the power to define yourself, or to RE-define yourself, however you CHOOSE. And not just for today, but to go back and redefine those moments in life when you have felt hurt, when you have hurt another - those times that maybe you are still holding on to, playing those old stories out over and over, perpetuating the hurt. Go back and find the gift in the lesson. Find the thing that has built your character, strength, empathy, compassion, and belief. Find it and feel grateful for the growth and lessons it has brought you. Look deep, it's there.

You can do it, no matter where you are starting from, no matter how far away it may feel...just make the choice, commit, and step forward.

> "People will forget what you said, people will forget what you did, but people will never forget how you made them feel."
>
> ~ Maya Angelou

CHAPTER FOUR

The Power Of Asking

By Tracy Sotirakis

Every photo of me as a child is the pretty much the same. Barely a smile, no teeth showing, hands clasped in front of me for protection. The classic shy child. I was the middle child with two sisters, and a scrawny little thing to top it off. All I wanted to do was play by myself in my room. Instead of hanging out with all the kids my age, I just wanted to listen to music and draw or go roller skating with my sisters. I had a couple of close friends as a child, but I was never that girl who was popular in school with tons of friends around all the time. I was the one who ate lunch by herself in the library if her one and only friend was out sick for the day.

School was my downfall. I hated it. There were many days that I simply could not go to school because it was too stressful, and it made me sick to my stomach. I would do anything to get out of going to school. I constantly lied to my mom and told her that I was sick. She could always see through my lies and would encourage me to just try and I would be okay, but I usually wasn't.

Anytime I was asked to speak out loud in school, I was filled with complete dread. It was crippling, heart stopping. It always felt like my stomach had dropped to my feet. My face would immediately turn the color of a tomato, no matter what, and being light-skinned with freckles, the intense redness was very obvious. I was smart enough to answer the questions, but I just didn't want everybody staring at me. I was so shy that it was painful. Every day at school was a struggle.

All my strong memories of grade school seem to revolve around my most embarrassing moments. My school had those old desks where you could flip the writing top open so you could store your books and pencils inside of it. I can't even count the amount of times that I opened up my desk and stuck my head inside to try to hide my bright red face. I would bury my head any time after reading out loud to the class or having to answer any of the teacher's questions.

The absolute worst thing for me was being on stage for the performances in the auditorium. My school had them *all* the time. One terrifying memory was when my class performed the musical *Grease*. My mom made my little pink poodle skirt, and I had to dance around and sing with my classmates. I hated every minute of it. As a tomboy, I was so embarrassed to not only be wearing a pink poodle skirt, but to be dancing in front of everybody, too. To this day, I refuse to watch the movie *Grease.* The memory of that school play is just too painful, and it makes me angry. My mom has a photo of me that was taken during a one of the many Christmas plays where I am supposed to be singing, but I just look absolutely horrified. I sure hope there are no photos of that stupid *Grease* play anywhere. They would probably end up in the garbage.

There wasn't any deep reason for the shyness. My childhood was happy. My family was loving. I had a few close friends. There was no major trauma in my life. I was simply born a shy, quiet introverted girl.

This cycle of shyness and embarrassment continued for my whole youth into high school. I landed my first job working in a little mall bakery when I was 15. As a chronically reserved young lady, taking customer's orders and having to interact with the public was my worst nightmare. What were they going to think of me? Would they think I was incompetent because I was so quiet?

After learning the regular customer's names and usual orders, I started to feel more comfortable around them. I began to smile more, actually showing my teeth. The more I smiled, the nicer the customers were to me, and it made my interaction with them easier. Every day was better than the last, and I even started enjoying going to work.

After I graduated high school, I moved and went to another state for college. School had never been anything that I loved, but I felt like I was supposed to go to college. That was what everybody did. The only subject that I enjoyed was art, so I half-assed my way through all my basic classes but really excelled in all of my art classes. I took drawing, painting, charcoal, and print-making classes and loved them. Biology, not so much. I had absolutely terrible grades in any class that wasn't art.

My college counselor advised me to pick a major and try to graduate. The only problem was that I had absolutely no drive to do so. Most of the people that I encountered in college said, "What are you going to do with an art degree? Teach art?" That was the most defeating thing that anybody had ever told me, and an astounding number of people said it to me over the years.

Living on my own, I still worked full-time through my college years so that I could pay my bills. My parents helped me out, but I needed income. I worked as a waitress and made a decent amount of money from my tips, but I felt like a loser with no direction in life. My friends and older sister had degrees that they were working towards and were excited about going to school. I dreaded it because I had no goals. I had repeatedly failed my math class to the point where the teacher actually told me not to take the class again.

Three years of suffering through the guilt of wasting thousands of dollars on horrible grades, I dropped out of school. I knew that I needed to do something about my education. One area that I'd always liked was the beauty industry. I went to one of the local beauty academies and had a meeting with one of their admissions counsellors to ask about their programs. She asked me about myself and then said, "If you can paint, you should do nails. You'll make great money." I figured that she knew what she was talking about, so I enrolled in the three-month nail technician program.

It was torture. I hated it. The smell of the chemicals gave me intense headaches. After getting my license, I was so completely disappointed in myself. Once again, I had wasted thousands of dollars on an education that I would never use. I continued to waitress and wallow in self-pity.

About six months after the nail school debacle, my sister had one of her famous barbecues. She had all sorts of interesting friends and there was usually a good number of people that attended. At the barbecue, I started chatting with a gentleman that I had never met before and had no idea how he was invited because he didn't know my sister. He was a photographer and had a photo studio locally. We spoke for a while and at the end of our conversation he said, "Well, if you can paint and draw and do nails, you should become a makeup artist." I tried to tell him that I didn't know a thing about makeup or what being a makeup artist entails. He said, "Buy some makeup and start doing makeup on my models for free, see if you like it." I told him I'd think about it and let him know.

I remember sitting on my couch later that night talking to my best friend on the phone. We discussed the fact that I didn't even wear much makeup, so I had no business doing anything like that. My self-esteem was at a low, and I felt totally defeated.

Overnight, something sparked inside and told me to do it. Take that chance. Try it. It couldn't be worse than all the other failures that I had gone through. I called the photographer the next day and let him know that I was in.

I bought a small basic makeup kit from the beauty school that I had previously attended. These were the days before YouTube and instructional videos on the internet, so I went to the library and checked out all the makeup books that I could. There weren't many. Those available were mostly about how to make someone look like a vampire for Halloween, but I studied them all.

The first time that I had to put makeup on a model, I was petrified. The makeup was absolutely horrible, but I kind of liked the whole process. I still have haunting visions of red blush that I applied too heavily on that poor first girl in the dark photo studio. It was pretty scary, but I continued to study and practice. I did makeup on all the photographer's models for free anytime there was a photo shoot, while continuing to waitress full-time. He was like a saint to let me learn and experiment on all of his gorgeous models.

Something clicked. I really enjoyed myself, and the work stimulated me. I had gone from painting and drawing on paper to painting on a face and creating something really beautiful. The better that I got at applying makeup, the more confidence I had. I made up my mind. I was going to stop wasting my time with my waitressing job and pursue makeup full-time. There weren't many makeup jobs in my area, except working at the mall or at other photo studios, so I did it all. I gained an extensive amount experience by taking any makeup job available, even the terrible ones. What I was still lacking was a formal education. It frightened me beyond belief that I might waste more money on schooling that I would never use, like in the past, but I knew that it had to be done so that I could really say that I was a professional and I had the education to back it up.

The makeup school that I was accepted into was in another state, California, about a four-hour drive from where I lived, with no traffic. Life was a little rough then. I went to school Monday through Thursday in California and worked at the mall in Nevada doing makeup Friday through Sunday. This went on for months and months, until I finally graduated from the makeup school. I'm not sure how many miles I put on my crappy car because the odometer went too high and finally broke.

All the driving at 2 a.m., the stress, and the long hours finally paid off. I was so proud of myself and all that I had accomplished. And to top it off, I was actually a very good makeup artist and excelled in school. All those classes in college that I thought were a complete waste of time really helped me understand things like color, texture, blending, and application with brushes.

For a shy girl, this type of a job may seem like a big stretch. Imagine being extremely introverted and doing a job where you have to be a foot away from a stranger and have a conversation with them—all while putting stuff on their face that they may or may not like. Absolutely horrifying.

Being a makeup artist requires a lot of talking and interaction, usually with someone that you have just met. It also requires you to make someone feel very comfortable around you. You can't act totally weird; it freaks clients out. I now work with actors, corporate clients and CEOs, famous people, brides, and just plain regular folks. I have to be able to have an engaging conversation with people from all walks of life, rich or poor, young and old, friendly to nasty.

The internet was my biggest helper in figuring out what to talk to my clients about. I began researching how to "chat." What I learned is that most people just really like to be asked about themselves. They like to talk to about their kids, their pets, their hobbies, where they went on vacation. Yes, you can talk about the weather, but the deeper that you go, the more you start to connect with people and learn about human behavior. The more you learn, the easier it is to interact with anybody that you come into contact with.

Sometimes I like to come up with a theme question. I had one freelance job where I was doing makeup for corporate head shot photos at a convention. Most of the people that we were photographing were from the Pacific coast of Canada. I've always heard that there are a lot of Sasquatch sightings there, so my theme question for the three-day job was, "Have you ever seen a Sasquatch?" You'd be surprised by how many interesting answers I got after asking this to 50 people over a three-day period. A crazy question like that got them to open up and helped to pass their time in the makeup chair quickly. It was rather amusing for me, too.

With extensive research and practicing what I have learned, my confidence has grown beyond my imagination. I have forced myself out of the crippling shyness that I suffered through as a child. My world has opened up immensely and I have learned so much from the wonderfully different people that I get to work with and talk to daily.

Now I want more. I want to move from being good to being great. I want to go from giving good service to giving outstanding service. Changing my mindset has really helped me move to a higher level of happiness in life. I focus on the positive now instead of dwelling on anything negative. I have changed my vision and now I think bigger. I don't have to go to work, I *get* to go to work.

I am eager to learn and experience things that I never would have faced as a child or young adult. I actually *want* to do things that scare me now. Not like bungee jumping off a bridge scary, but things like public speaking, which can be debilitating for a lot of people.

The opportunity came up for me to speak about makeup techniques at a large beauty convention. The little shy girl inside of me said, "NO WAY! ARE YOU KIDDING ME? GO ON A STAGE?" The new me said, "Sure, what's the worst that's going to happen? It'll be a great experience and I'll learn something new." The first time I did it, I will admit, I was very nervous. I didn't eat that morning, my stomach felt like it was going to explode. Getting up on that stage for the first time was the scariest thing that I have ever done. I know I said some stupid things, probably talked really fast and just generally looked very uncomfortable, but I made it through—alive. It was the most empowering feeling in the world.

The next year, when the same beauty convention came around, I asked if I could speak again. To my surprise, they said yes. I now continue to speak and teach with them every chance I get. So, to all those fools who asked me in college, "What are you going to do with an art degree, teach art?" I say yes! I do teach art now, and I love it!

Asking to speak again at this convention made me realize that asking for something you desire is the first step in moving yourself to the next level. If we never ask for what we want, we are probably not going to get it. I have found that the more I ask for, the more I receive. Sometimes I am told no, but usually I am told yes.

Asking for small things at first really helps in building confidence to ask for big things. I ask for samples at every beauty store I go to. When checking in to a hotel, I ask for a room with a great view. I ask for anything better. I ask for what I desire. All of this is done with eye contact and a smile, which helps boost confidence and makes you look sincere.

Many years ago, I was booked to do makeup for a high profile professional speaker that was holding a four-day seminar. After doing research on him, I discovered that he was extremely intelligent and had a no-nonsense, blunt personality. He was not a soft cuddly kitty, and I had to put makeup on his face for his speaking engagement on stage in front of thousands of people. The nervousness and fright of my childhood came back with a vengeance.

I bought a smart little business suit and some high heels to look the part. I called him Sir but otherwise barely spoke to him. I was so scared. While doing his makeup the first day, he told me that he usually fires all of his makeup artists for not doing a good job or for saying something inappropriate to him. Great! That didn't help things.

By the fourth day, he hadn't fired me, and I was a little more comfortable around him. I sat backstage the whole time and listened to him speak. He was a wonderful speaker and I really admired how comfortable and engaging he was on stage. I learned that he traveled all around the United States and spoke to large audiences a few times a year. I knew that I wanted to be his personal makeup artist for his speaking engagements. Why not? He was wealthy; if he liked me, his company would fly me around. But how do you ask someone like that without losing your cool and looking like a complete idiot?

I wrote out some notes and practiced what I was going to say beforehand. When I saw him for a makeup touch-up after our lunch break, I took a deep breath and said, "Sir, I would like to be your personal makeup artist and travel around with you." He immediately said, "Yes. Talk to my secretary and make it happen." Wow, my heart almost stopped. He said yes! I went into the bathroom and did the dance of joy.

What I learned from our interaction was that I had gained his respect for asking to be his makeup artist. He never would have offered it. He wanted me to ask him, to show that I desired and valued the position. I now work with him a few times a year, and I am a highly respected member of his personal crew.

From these work and life experiences that I have forced upon myself, the timid shy girl of the past is pretty much gone. Very rarely do I ever get the red tomato face of embarrassment. Of course, there may be certain situations and people that I am still a little shy around, but I don't beat myself up over it or let it engulf me. I remind myself of all that I have accomplished, and I snap out of the shyness instantly.

My metamorphosis is irreversible. I will never go back to being the way that I was as a young girl. I have come too far. It has been a slow process, and it definitely did not happen overnight. Looking back, I am dramatically different than I was at 7, 18, or 30. Sometimes I wish that I'd had this knowledge when I was younger. It definitely would have made things easier. But I know I had to go through the process to be where I am today. I am proud that I never gave up. I kept going and turned my obstacles into opportunities. I will always thank my parents, sisters, and friends for their support in all of my crazy adventures.

Through dedication, research, and practice, I have turned myself into someone who I am honored to be, and I have found my dream job. My goals and aspirations for the future include climbing higher in my much-loved career and taking all the scary challenges that come my way. I don't know where my path may lead, but I know it's going to be wonderful!

> "Living in the light of eternity changes your priorities."
> ~ Rick Warren

CHAPTER FIVE

Ultimate Healing

By Tom Wind

Mundane Reality

"I'll have another one!" I shout out to the waiter, pointing at my Negroni. I had a difficult day. I deserve it.

I don't enjoy drinking anymore; it has become as dull and depressive as everything else I do. I guess I am only here at my neighborhood bar in Four Seasons because I don't feel like going home and facing my girlfriend, Kamile, after we had another argument this morning. To be honest, I don't even remember what we were arguing about. It is not about her. It's about me.

I just feel so tired, overworked, and overwhelmed with my business and my life itself. I am burned out. I need a break. I feel I am not able to cope with the levels of stress and anxiety I am experiencing, and I need to check out and have some time to myself if I am to continue this way. As an entrepreneur, all I do is work to add value for my customers, earn money, and spend it all on things that don't even matter. How did I end up this way? I am not sure if anything I do has a deeper meaning whatsoever. I am tired of my relationship; it has become such hard work. It feels I have fallen into the trap of society's doctrines and have ended up following the norm like everybody else. I feel I am doing what my family, friends, and society tell me to do, which leaves me living a life which is not my own. I don't even know what I like. I don't feel like I know myself or who I have become.

What do I want to do? This question always brings me confusion, and I have never found the time to answer this, as I am always too busy. Busy playing roles which I have adopted for myself.

There's got to be more to life than this.

***

This is not a summary of books I have read on self-development, transformation, or spirituality. This is a testimony of what I have experienced searching for the most effective personal healing for my body, mind, and soul, which led me to a deep transformational journey of self-actualization. I have become an ayahuasca shaman (plant medicine healer), established a retreat center in Bali, and for almost two years lived a life of transformational change daily and then left it all behind to pursue a life of truth and freedom. I challenge you to have an open mind, as this chapter has nothing to do with any religion or sect and instead is a personal journey of self-discovery, searching for an elixir of life—Ultimate Healing.

Some of the experiences I am about to share are quite out there and may be difficult to relate to. However, I believe for each one of you there was a time in your life when you'd had enough and knew that you had to change. My journey is all about change. As you are reading this book, you must have some degree of desire to transform that which no longer serves you, and my intention is to point you towards the direction I have found to be the ultimate path to freedom, joy, and lasting transformation.

As a former shaman and someone who has organized transformational retreats for a living, I have come across many non-traditional ways to heal the body, mind, and soul. What I discovered is that many of them do more harm than good. I understand my chapter will face a lot of resistance and hostility from different healers out there, most of whom are probably just trying to help people while doing the best they can. It is not my intention to offend anyone or condemn their practices. However, I believe that we have the right to know the truth behind some of the movements happening in the world right now, movements which basically aim to deceive us into a life of New Age slavery, and I will share exactly how I discovered this hidden mystery, much to my complete surprise.

Mystical Experience

As we walked into this beautiful hilltop lounge in West Koh Phangan, Thailand, I was filled with fear of stepping into the unknown. Kamile and I had agreed to take a magic mushroom shake, a hallucinogenic drink, and see if this intimate soul-opening experience would bring us closer together and help us sort out our relationship issues.

Not sure how much time had passed or what had happened, I found myself lying on the beach staring at the sky and witnessing things my mind could not comprehend. I had never believed in any supernatural stories and was convinced that this reality is all there is. My logical brain was exploding, as what I was seeing was outside of my ordinary world, or at least outside of what I had been conditioned to see.

Beings of light descended from the skies in human bodies just like yours and mine. I shook my head to wake up from this hallucination, but they were still there observing me and trying to communicate. I could sense their wisdom and intellect. These were saints and sages from other worlds. A huge image of Machu Picchu appeared in the skies, and I instantly knew that I had to go there.

Do I Stay Or Do I Go?

I was no longer the same person I had been before the trip to Thailand. I could not stay at the office and pretend that everything was okay. I was anxious; my mind was driving me crazy. All I could think about was going to Peru. I could see clearly how dysfunctional and vain my life was and how to fill that emptiness I was feeling inside, the emptiness I had built a fake identity around in order to validate myself. I had to find out who was the person inside, who was the real me.

But who was I to take this journey? I was just a regular guy with no talents, no supernatural capabilities. Two weeks earlier, I'd had no idea that other beings existed and that there were other forms of life out there. I had commitments to my girlfriend and to my staff and clients here. I sensed that I could lose it all. I was scared. What if I took the call to Peru and went through whatever I had to go through and ended up losing everything I had worked for so hard for 30 years of my life? My business, my status and reputation—what if I decided to donate all of it to some charities and ended up living alone on the streets or, even worse, in a mental institution as an insane person? That part of the world is really dangerous, and stepping into the unknown and unexplored territories of other dimensions could be lethal. I had faced too many challenges in my life already, and I felt that I was at a safe and comfortable place right then, so why risk all that?

But, then again, the thought that I had to go to Peru wouldn't leave me. I could not continue living the way I was living before and expect a different result. I guess getting stuck in one place and living a boring and monotonous life would become my reality if I didn't go.

I've always had the desire to change, transform, and become a part of something greater than me.

I was going!

Entering Behind The Veil

We were leaving the stony streets of Cusco and heading towards the mountaintops of the Andes. All I knew was that there was a shaman out there who would help me cross into unknown realms where possibilities were limitless, where danger was real and not coming back was always a possibility. I should have been scared. But I was not. For some reason, this Peruvian man named Pedro, who was wearing a headband with a few feathers weaved into his hair, filled me with confidence, which is quite unusual seeing the way he drove his 20-year-old WV Beatle with reckless abandon and considering that he spoke no English.

This very tall and well-built Native American man walked into the tepee. I could sense his power and confidence. He definitely knew what he was doing. A few prayers later, he passed me the cup of thick brown liquid.

I stopped for a second. Was I really doing this?

I downed the medicine in one go. It tasted disgusting. I would have vomited if I'd had anything in my stomach. I hadn't eaten much for days due to the food poisoning I had experienced earlier in the week and altitude sickness from being over 3km above sea level. So, I was physically weak, but I guessed that was part of the journey. I surrendered to the experience, knowing that I had to do this or else I would never know what my life could have become. This is what I thought to myself.

Enduring hours of intense shaking, vomiting, facing my biggest fears, and letting go of everything I knew of myself and the reality I was living in... at the end I had no idea who I was or if I'd ever even existed.

I died. I checked out; I left my body and felt myself being pulled upwards towards the light. I was becoming the light myself. I was filled with peace and bliss. I was with God. There was no separation between us. We were one. For a moment I became God myself. I experienced oneness with everything. This felt like coming back home.

At that enlightening point, I could access Godly wisdom and remember everything about my life: every person I had ever met, every book I had read, and I could understand the meaning of it all, the story of my life, which I could now see for the first time. It was the journey of my soul where I'd had to take some twists and turns in order to learn and grow. I also saw myself going off track, sabotaging myself with alcohol, drugs, and meaningless sexual relationships. I saw the amounts of pain and suffering I had caused others and myself. These had to be healed.

Reluctantly, I descended back to my body and opened my eyes. I was back and not too happy about it, as I would have preferred to have stayed in that blissful state of meditation.

This near-death experience gave me a purpose, a clear vision of my life: to heal myself, heal others, and eventually to go back to that state of bliss. For the first time in my life, I knew exactly what I had to do and where I was going to end up. I was not scared of anything, as I had already experienced what death feels and I quite liked it.

As incredible as this experience was, this was not a true enlightenment, as I learned later on in my journey. At that time, I truly believed that this was the peak of what this life is all about. But little did I know, this was just a mere shadow of what's to come.

The Road Of Trials

Where am I? Who are these people? I started questioning myself sitting in a circle of shamans, witches, and hippie-looking healers—all dressed in white—those who call themselves the spiritual elite of Bali—leaders of the awakened community. To me, this looked more like a pagan ritual than a gathering of consciously evolved spiritual leaders. It was like turning back time and going back to making magic, attuning oneself with the forces of nature, worshiping wind, fire, earth, spirit animals...everything but our actual Creator. These people looked more confused to me than anyone I had met in London or Dubai. Had I really left my comfortable life behind to come here to Bali, the epicenter of New Age healing and spiritual awakening, to find this charade? Instead of alcohol or drugs, people here were getting high on plant medicine, cacao, breathing, fasting, drumming, etc., to reach higher states of consciousness and come closer to their "Divine natures."

Was this really just an unconscious charade, or was there something deeper and more meaningful happening out here? Most of these healers looked like they had completely lost touch with this reality. They seemed to be in desperate need of healing themselves. I would not trust them to perform any of their healing rituals on me, that's for sure.

Even so, I had noticed a few healers demonstrating some type of spiritual arrogance and pride about them. However, there was certain peace radiating from them too. Their eyes were deep, full of wisdom, and I could sense their spiritual power even by looking at them from afar. I had to find out what they were on. I had to get behind the scenes.

I had no fear; I was determined there was no stopping me. I had to find the Ultimate Healing. This courage and enthusiasm led me to trying out everything that was giving any lasting results. But the more practices I followed, the more medicine ceremonies and New Age healing circles I attended, the more pain and suffering I had to deal with...this started to look like a vicious cycle with no end to it. I needed to go deeper and figure out what it would take to truly heal. I needed to know what the world's wisest masters know. It did not matter if I would have to go to the other side of the world to find it.

And indeed, that's where it was: exactly at the opposite side of the globe—the Amazon Jungle—the most powerful healing experience on this planet, or so I thought at that time—master class for ayahuasca shamans, the Peruvian Dieta. It meant six weeks of fasting leading up to the 10-day secluded retreat in the Amazon Jungle with experienced native shamans. In complete silence, I worked with ayahuasca and seven other master teacher plants daily in order to heal and purge all my past emotional pain and hurt. It looked like the real deal, a complete restoration of my body and soul, a chance for a new life. Unexpectedly, with this experience the door to the spiritual dimension was opened so wide that, at times, I was not able to come back to this reality and relate to the events happening here. I was on the edge of going crazy.

Luckily enough, or so I thought at the time, God sent me a master, a Buddhist monk who for the past 15 years had been specializing in enlightenment and esoteric studies. He noticed my spiritual potential and with daily practices helped me to integrate all these powerful energies into my body. Little did I know back then, this would put me on a dangerous path of enlightenment, would open the doors to other worlds of insane wisdom, and would initiate me into the hierarchy of ascended masters who would introduce me to their deceptive future plans for the Earth and Humanity. I share this in detail in my book.

Becoming A Master

Sun gazing is yet another ancient spiritual practice which leads to abundant health and enlightenment, as I thought back then. Here I was greeting the morning sun overlooking the retreat center my partner and I had now opened, a place where people could experience true awakening. It seemed like the future vision I received during my second visit to the Amazon Jungle had become my reality, as I had created an actual luxury retreat center in a most wonderful riverside location in south Bali where real transformational change happened daily. Not only that, I also became a disciple of the Great White Brotherhood, a spiritual hierarchy of ascended masters, accepted my calling and began to follow the path of shamanism, and, after a number of extra visits to the Amazon Jungle and years of study and practice, I was also initiated by my master shaman who happened to be one of the most respected Peruvian shamans worldwide. I officially became a shaman who held ceremonial retreats to help people heal.

I was living out my purpose. I had finally healed and now I was able to heal others. We had high-level businessmen from Europe and the US coming over here with their management teams for secret transformational retreats with the medicine, all paying tens of thousands of dollars for the experience.

I should have been happy, but I was not. Was there something I'd missed or had not yet understood?

I still couldn't get the previous day's conversation with my friend Michael out of my head.

What did he mean? "Christ is the strongest entity out there and the only true healer."

How would he know? I was the shaman and I was committing all that I was to helping others heal. I was connected to the best healers representing the most effective healing modalities, and I thought I was working with the strongest spirits and that God was behind my back to help all these wonderful souls heal and find their purposes.

Michael simply listened to my crazy journeys to other spiritual worlds, where I got to travel frequently due to my profession, and all he said was, "Try connecting to Christ. He is the strongest out there."

Certainty, love, and peace radiated from him when he said it. That's exactly what I needed in my life right then.

I soon discovered that it is not the shaman who does the healing but the entity behind him. So, is it really the shamans who control these powers, or are they led to believe they control them but instead are just the puppets in a much greater scheme that they, being the tools, do not comprehend?

In my book, I unpack this deception in more depth and share the three scariest secrets of shamanism: the life I have lived and the experiences I had to go though and the price I have paid for the spiritual wisdom and powers I received. I will be sharing all this to make sure that you become fully aware of the dangers involved if choosing to participate in one of these sacred medicine ceremonies arranged by the "trusted shaman."

I was led to believe that what I was doing was fulfilling the plan of God. I was helping others to deal with their issues and to transform their pain into love. However, I would see the same people turning up for the healing ceremonies month after month. They were becoming more open, friendly, more accepting of each other, but were they really getting the Ultimate Healing?

I could see people getting off their addictions and compulsive disorders, but at what cost?

The Darkest Cave

As a shaman, I did not know at the time that I was getting myself into a dangerous game of spiritual wisdom with strings attached. The further I went into the self-discovery journey, the more attached I became to the power working behind me. I was losing my life force energy, did not care for myself anymore, and was totally oblivious to what was unfolding. All I did was serve humanity, which meant I was doing what my spiritual masters and gurus were telling me to do. For someone who has not yet experienced a real conversation with God, it felt that I was hearing the thoughts of God and serving Him and His spiritual hierarchy of saints and masters. So, in my mind, serving these hierarchical beings meant serving God. But I wasn't. The deeper I travelled into my spiritual path, the less love I was feeling. I had become very peaceful and wise but, at the same time, emotionless and cold.

With each initiation, I was becoming wiser and more powerful. At the peak of my power and during the 7th initiation within the spiritual hierarchy, I was then introduced to the concept that everything is God, which included all good and all evil. I was shown that I had to accept both as equally important in order to grow. I was now the creator of my reality and I would decide for myself what is good and what is evil.

What followed next left me totally gob-smacked and completely shaken by the experience.

After the 7th initiation, during one of my spiritual travels with the plant medicine, I arrived in a world which had no love. I was shocked by how this world had no love at all and was run purely on intellect, otherwise called "will-of-god" energy. This was the Shambhala world I was hearing about from my enlightenment master. The laws, which governed that planet and the beings, all ran on pure intellect and they had no warmth, tenderness, or love.

I was scared to realize how much wisdom I was able to access and how much I could create purely with the power of intellect and science. I was able to comprehend how the creation happens and how to manifest different realities. Yet there was no tenderness. There was no humanity, and there was no love whatsoever.

Till then, I had been carrying the energy of love and wisdom, reporting to and serving the masters of the Great White Brotherhood. This looked like I was being taken to the next level without even considering what I wanted. I had never expected that my devotional service-based spiritual journey would lead me to a place where I was requested to detach from love itself, that love was actually considered to be a feeling designed for the lesser-evolved human souls and not a spiritual master like me. It was really hard for me to comprehend this, as I have always thought of God as love.

Things did not end there. I was now at the most shocking experience of my life, where I had my "judgment day" and I was reminded of all the wisdom and power I have received to heal myself and others. I was pressured by these beings and was feeling the heaviness of the debt I had accumulated from the wisdom they gave me. And now, for all these superpowers and wisdom, in order for me to progress to the next level, to my biggest shock, I had to accept and worship Satan as my god and creator.

I understood that the path I was walking was not at all what I had thought it was. After the near-death experience (the false enlightenment), I forgot about myself and my family and surrendered my life to serving this false god. Satan ruled this incredible power structure of alleged masters, saints, and very advanced beings. Shockingly, I found myself working, without even knowing it, against the True Creator within the armies of His enemy, which I soon discovered and will be sharing about later in this chapter.

Revelation

At this critical point of my human and spiritual life, I reached a dead end; nothing could set me free from the unconscious commitments I'd made to serve these ascended masters and medicine spirits. I was crushed. As the last resort, I fell on my knees and cried for Jesus Christ to come and save me.

Just like a wind, He entered my full body, and I became more alive than ever before. His energy feels so pure, clean, and perfect. My throat dried out. He touched my heart, and I instantly started weeping like a small child who had been scared and lost in the wilderness and now was found by his father. A sense of peace and knowing that everything is okay penetrated my body. This incredible love of God filled every cell of my being. I cried from joy that Jesus came. I thought I was forsaken, but now I know that He cares for me and I am worthy of His love. The love and wisdom I came across before was nothing like the joy, love, perfection, and freedom I am experiencing now. This Love of Christ is so much greater than anything else I have known before; it feels like butterflies inside making my heart sing.

All creation is here to worship Him. I can hear flowers, trees, birds, animals, and wind whispering His name. Now I know that he is God. All these other times in my journeys, a lesser being would flee in fear if a more powerful being appeared. But this time I know that they are here to glorify His presence. This is His world.

All my worries get transformed into solutions instantly. Suddenly everything becomes clear. I am filled with courage, and I know the steps needed to reach my salvation. I know what I must do to cleanse my soul and, most importantly, I am 100% sure that this is the Truth I have been seeking for so long. I know that no one else can love me and care for me more than Jesus Christ. Only He can heal me, free me from my past, and transform me forever.

I know in my heart that He is the reason I live. Jesus claimed to be the way, the Truth, and the life, and now I have experienced that this is reality and have tasted the love and perfection of His presence.

Greater Understanding

After experiencing Christ, it became obvious that there is actually no need to enter behind the veil in order to heal my soul, because behind the veil are these worlds of fallen beings and entities. They are called different names by different people: ascended masters, gurus, saints, ancestors, ancient wise ones, aliens, gods and goddesses, reptilians, fallen angels, or simply daemons. They seem to control what's behind the veil at this stage and time and they all seem to need our life force to keep fueling their worlds.

I realized that the real value is to be here at this moment and bring the love and kindness into this moment I am experiencing now. This physical world is where we are meant to be. We are in this world for a reason; we are having this life and these experiences for a reason. I found that God is guiding us through our hearts in this reality. I learned that many of the practices that I did in order to open my third eye were guiding me away from God. All these medicine ceremonies and meditations were actually guiding me into the worlds controlled by these fallen angels. And this was the reason why, with vivid visions, it was so easy for the enemy to deceive me and so many of the healers I worked with. These were Satan's kingdoms we were entering, as he controls these worlds, dimensions, and realities.

The light of Christ gave me an understanding that these worlds are not what they seem. My friend Michael told me a long time ago, but I did not know. I hadn't experienced it for myself at that time and was convinced that what I saw was the truth for me. But it wasn't. Now I know that there is only one Truth, and I only discovered it because I experienced Christ for myself. I now can see what is in those worlds in a way I could not see before. I realize that these spiritual beings were not there to help me; they needed my energy and wanted to control my mind in order to fulfill their agenda on this planet.

The spiritual challenge, which I failed to overcome at the time, was the superego thought that I am better than others, that I am a master and I can heal others. Because of the belief that I was a master, I made it so easy for these beings to deceive me. They just had to be there as my masters, and my hunger for wisdom opened the doors for them to use me.

Especially in these days, the reason for the New Age movement is to feed us these thoughts of being masters, healers, and eventually becoming God to pull us towards the direction of spiritual initiations and enlightenment, which is a lie. I have taken this path and, as I shared, faced a shocking discovery at the end of the trail.

We each have our human free will to exercise; we have so many choices but only one true choice: Jesus Christ. Now I know that there are ultimately only two options: to choose God or choose against God. If I am not choosing Jesus Christ to live through me and protect me, then I am opening myself up to all other energies to use me and work through me as they wish. Now that I understand this, I can only experience true freedom when living in Christ.

So, I realize now that the Ultimate Healing is the healing of the relationship between me and God, Jesus Christ.

Greater Transformation

My intention was to heal and find the Ultimate Healing which could be shared with others. The journey took me to live in Europe, the Middle East, South America, and Asia and to study most of the religions, New Age philosophies, and movements. I learned ancient wisdom from native people, got into esoteric science, and followed the path of enlightenment, and most practices were actually taking me away from God, leaving me with less life-force energy and less desire to act and create. It was only by experiencing Christ and discerning the energies and entities behind all these movements that I could be led to the Truth: Ultimate Healing with Christ.

It took me a while to digest this experience and understand the meaning and the dangers of the path I was walking before. Having Jesus Christ as a contrast frame, I can now understand these other energies so much better, see through the lies, and sense the Truth beyond the veils they present.

My first ayahuasca experience, which I thought to be a near-death experience, enlightenment, and coming back to God, was actually me experiencing the realm of the enemy. This blissful state was a lie; that is not our end goal. I was shown how much hurt and pain I had to clear and how much healing I needed. I was guided to create a luxury retreat center, to become a shaman and serve his plan of "saving humanity".

I realized how deceptive and sophisticated these beings are; I experienced all these ascended masters as beings of light. They were filled with love and some of them had certain holiness around them. They were compassionate, took time to build my trust, and even performed physical healings. All that time, I believed I was healing myself and that my consciousness was expanding much faster than everybody else's. In reality, I was being guided away from God and away from my true purpose for being here. During all this time, I was functioning in my body and others saw me as someone powerful, wise, and financially independent when, in reality, I was becoming a New Age slave without even knowing it.

I have since transformed from someone who had lost his free will and served the hierarchy of Satan to a follower of

Jesus Christ, because I have experienced His light and love. After what I have witnessed in the other worlds, I needed to know if there was a way out of this confusion and madness. And Jesus Christ showed me the way. This was not a one-off experience of Christ. This started the Ultimate Healing process, freeing my soul from bondage and building my relationship with Jesus as my Savior and Lord.

I left my past life as a shaman and transformational retreat center owner to pursue a life of Truth. Jesus Christ has paid my debt and washed off all of my past hurt and pain and has allowed me to experience what it really feels like to live in freedom.

I have found that Jesus Christ is the only power which can truly heal the soul and free it from invaders and overcome Satan. I have since performed a number of deliverance services in which I have witnessed the true power of the name of Jesus. I have seen spiritually possessed and ill people getting healed instantly by His presence. He is the way. He is the Ultimate Power in this Universe.

Freedom To Live

Living with Christ has transformed my everyday life, which is now filled with liveliness and freedom to express myself. He is empowering me to act on inspiration with peace and confidence and to create the life of my dreams. I used to work for money. Now I work for the joy of it. I travel to different countries sharing my story, consulting clients, and helping them to experience and reconnect to Jesus Christ.

I am now filled with the courage to act and express myself freely without the need to overthink or fully rely on my past experiences, connections, money, or the life conditions I was given. Now I live daily on inspiration, which leaves me living a life of adventure and joy, something I have always dreamed of. I learned to live in the now and enjoy this moment like never before. Clarity and distinct separation from my mind allows me to do what I want and to use my mind as a tool to get me where I decide to go. I can create what I decide to create and not the other way around as it used to be.

I used to be at war with myself, constantly feeling lost and confused. Now I live in certainty, with a clear mind and trust that God is behind me in anything I do. I used to be overworked and tired and did not have time for my girlfriend or my personal life. Now I am energized. I get to spend quality time with her each day, and I feel physically better and so much more active than I ever felt before and, most importantly, I have the energy to do the things I love.

I remember when I was not able to commit in my intimate relationship; sometimes I would get angry wanting to end it for no reason. Once I began living with Christ, I found that all of the anger and pain that had been inside of me just left. I used to be cold, rarely expressing my emotions and feelings. Now I am much more emotional. My partner, Kamile, has noticed the change, and this has really allowed us to have more intimacy. We are now happily married and have a beautiful daughter.

The transformation did not stop with only myself; my family and many close friends and clients were also inspired by the deep transformation they witnessed in my life. They, too, were able to reconnect to Christ and are now experiencing a much more peaceful and joyful life.

Taste The Elixir Of Life

If you've found that my chapter resonated with you and you would like to discover more about my findings, I would love for you to continue the journey with me and read *Shaman's Journey Back to Christ.* Go to www.tom-wind.com/books to get access to my main book, in which I go much deeper into what I have discovered throughout my entire spiritual journey and openly disclose the dangers of following certain practices like meditation, yoga, energy healing, medicine ceremonies, fortune tellers, New Age movements, etc. I share the names of deceptive entities I was working with, whose energies are manifesting very rapidly in today's western world, and I disclose their hidden agenda for the Christian church and humanity. What I have mentioned here in this chapter is just a tip of the iceberg of what I reveal in my book.

I am not here to change someone's religious beliefs or convince anyone that Jesus Christ is real. My intention is to speak the Truth into the hearts of those who are ready to hear.

I am here for those of you who have Faith in God and desire to fulfill your highest destinies.

"The best way to take care of the future is to take care of the present moment."

~ Thich Nhat Hanh

CHAPTER SIX

The Presents in Presence

By Mia Tolis

"Why is life so complicated and complex?" I would often ask myself. In reflection, this was such a disempowering question to ask oneself. Asking "why" questions, I have learnt, only spirals your self-worth, self-hope, and self-confidence downward. It also presupposes life is complicated and complex. Such a limited belief. Perhaps a better question is, "How can I appreciate even more the simplicity of life?" Now, that would be more empowering and inspiring. It has been a long journey to bring me to this point right now.

Life is simple, and I was making it complex. I was tired, and I was burning out from the presumed complexity of life and its challenges. I realized that I was making life too complicated. I was choosing life to be complicated for me. Decisions and choices were difficult, as I was making the decision processes cumbersome and complex. I was an overthinker. I would live in the past and compare all the good times from then to the problems I was facing in the now. I would always second-guess everything and expect the worst, enslaved by the past. I would take things personally, set high standards, and strive for perfection whilst constantly criticizing and questioning my efforts. I felt tense most of the time and couldn't switch off and relax.

Making life complex was an understatement, as I was consistently wired to find the next thing to do mentally and physically. Running to find the next thing to do, mentally and physically. I had to always **do**; I could not just **be**. This was how I was living my life. I was a "human doing" and not a "human being." With all the overthinking processing through my head, it would naturally materialize into my physical reality. I was focussing on many things. My actions were a result of what I was focussing on or what I thought I was focussing on. My thoughts were scattered, and my energy was feeding off them, creating multiple scenarios which were all bumping into each other, causing distractions, digressions, and diversions. As a result, I was focussing on many things and I later realized this was not living with focus.

Even conducting the simplest of tasks would digress to starting new ones before completing the old. I was constantly adding to that dreaded To-Do list which never seemed to end. Despite achieving and fulfilling these tasks, there was always a feeling of emptiness.

This void needed to be constantly filled with doing—doing to impress, to fulfil the need of significance, doing to connect with others, to fulfil the need of love and connection. Certainty and control were driving my motivation, and I needed that control. Otherwise I couldn't function. As a result, I created lists for everything. I even had a Master List to control the lists. I was living with overwhelm and the lists were the only way to relinquish this. This was an illusion and belief which I later learnt was totally unrealistic.

I realized I was living with a scarce mindset. Scarcity was my fear of running out of time, not having enough, and essentially not being enough. I felt there wasn't enough time to achieve, which created a feeling of uncertainty. I was not comfortable with this level of uncertainty, but the lists created a coping mechanism fulfilling my certainty. I was like a dog trying to catch its tail, running around in circles and never able to catch it, or running around in the shape of the infinity symbol, creating an infinite loop destined to never end. This was never going to stop unless I took control. Well, if it were I who created these feelings, then it was only I who could control the feelings.

Attending seminars, constantly reading, having a curious mind, and having a thirst for knowledge fuelled the behaviour. This enabled me to continue the path of growth since my early childhood, drawing on recollections of learnings from the age of five which I still fondly remember. Knowledge influenced me to the point where I became a passionate adult educator and teacher. To this day, I love sharing and supporting others with my knowledge and wisdom, making a positive difference in people's lives. Contributing my time to organisations connected me to others and fulfilled the need to give back to the community. I was addicted to life in the doing but something did not feel right. I was not happy and wanted the merry-go-round I was on to slow down.

I had achieved success in my earlier years in the areas of receiving educational awards and financial success investing in properties and owning franchise businesses. I had been married for over thirty years to a wonderful, patient, handsome man, raised two beautiful successful young men, was a proud wife and mum, supportive daughter, sister, sister-in-law, aunt, and a very loyal friend within my inner circle. I was a great supporter to everyone, and all of this was part of my success story.

Inner happiness had eluded me. The reason for the emotional marathon I was running seemed to be that I was chasing this inner happiness. In reflection, I recognized this was due to the constant noise and activity in my mind. Over the years, I had learnt that mindset is everything. I had to slow down the mind and focus. Something had to change. Changing my thoughts, in turn, would change my life.

Here is where my story begins. As a five-year-old, I innocently did not have these feelings of fear, overwhelm, and uncertainty. I loved my five-year-old self, a happy and content little girl. The play shelf I had in my room by my window included puzzles, books, a blackboard with coloured chalk, a doll with her assorted wardrobe of clothes, and a fawn-coloured teddy bear given to me for my first birthday and proudly still is with me. One of my most prized possessions was my bedside lamp of Mother Mary surrounded with soft pastel-coloured lights, which I treasured. I was blessed to have a mum and dad who I knew loved me, a house to live in, clothes and a well-stocked refrigerator full of food available at any time to eat from. This was my little world where I was content and very happy.

So, what happened? I had all of this and even more as an adult and was not happy, forever reaching out and wanting more. I knew I was lost. I had to find me again. Where had she gone? I knew she was somewhere deep in my soul, and with my greatest gift of intuition, I trusted she was there; she was still within me! The little girl who always knew she was gifted.

Growing up in an emotionally charged family, an environment where emotions were always expressed no matter what was said, was both empowering and disempowering. We were the most transparent family I knew when it came to expressing our views, emotions, and opinions. It was interesting to notice this pattern of behaviour within our family, and from both sides of the family, maternal and paternal: strong personalities constantly projecting their views and opinions. The only way to survive was to join them; otherwise one would not be heard.

The upside to this behaviour was, we always knew where we stood with each other, and we interpreted this as being honest. Being transparent, for us, was being honest. Later in life, I learnt this was honesty and transparency from one person's perspective. This behaviour and mindset of transparency within the family lay the foundation of honesty as the family's most respected value.

As the years went on, the house became noisy and busy. There were always people, guests, activities, and family dramas occurring, so the pattern of behaviour continued from one generation to the next. Years later, as a result of this conditioning, I recognized this pattern. I became aware of my thoughts having become noisy and busy. I needed to change. I needed to take action for my own life and for the generations which followed.

Life was like living in a shaken snow globe with all the snow falling in front of the figurine within the globe. Clarity was consistently blurred, and direction and focus were unclear. The noise and busyness of life and the lack of clarity to live through the noise and denseness were forever challenging. New skills were required to deal with the new challenges. So, I went in search, knowing my greatest resource was my resourcefulness, and I was quite resourceful in learning about human behaviour in which this noise became even busier. Once again, the dog chasing its tail and the infinity pattern were occurring in my life.

This pattern continued to occur throughout my life. Every gift has a problem, and the other side to this is every problem has a gift. The snow globe and the noise within the snow globe had to settle, which would enable clarity and focus. Focus would enable presence, and presence would enable the awareness of my emotions. This control and letting go of my emotions would eventually lead to freedom and a feeling of peace and inner happiness that I was in search of.

I realized I had been living in the snow globe without clarity, focus, and presence; I was scattered like the snowflakes falling. I needed to become less scattered and to become focussed on the present. As a five-year-old, I had that clarity, focus, and presence and, as such, have many clear and vivid memories of that time, memories of a happy and free little girl who was quiet and gifted. In fact, she was so quiet that her parents would even lose her in the home and would come looking for her. She was quiet, within her own mind, living within her own world. The noise was missing, and her mind had clarity. She was a high-achieving student where her gifts were presence, clarity, curiosity, and her thirst for knowledge. It was during her teen years when the emotions took control.

As an adult without presence, clarity, and focus, there are many years I cannot recall due to the busyness and emotions that were driving me. To find this inner happiness, I needed to let go of the noise. I had to slow down. I knew I had to peel back the layers just like those of an onion.

I realized my emotions were controlling me and I was not controlling my emotions. I was burning out. Emotions had been my energy. Learning that everything is energy and focussing by being present, I was able to be aware and harness this energy, channeling it towards achieving more with less emotional energy and to live in the present with inner happiness. Happiness was always there; I had just forgotten how to get there. Transformation occurs when one reaches threshold.

As a young child and teenager, I remember always being an observer and would look for the learnings. As an adult, I learnt to live by the mantra, "Everything happens for a reason. What can I learn from this, and how can I use the learning moving forward?" An example of applying the learnings was, as an eighteen-year-old, whilst on my bi-annual visit to the dentist, he noticed a tiny cavity behind my front tooth and told me he would fill it at my next appointment. Acting on it six months later eventually resulted in the tooth requiring root canal treatment, as the cavity's depth had reached the nerve. Five years later, an implant was required at a time when implants were not a common procedure. Decades later, thankfully, the learnings obtained from my dental experience saved my life. In a doctor's surgery, I had insisted on having two moles cut out from my back when the doctor was not recommending for them to be removed. I persisted in having them both removed, and the results from the biopsy returned stating two Stage two Skin Cancer Melanomas. I thank the dentist who, years prior, had decided not to fill the small cavity at the back of my front tooth when I felt it should have been done. Being present, with clarity, and being focussed without emotions years later enabled me to apply the learnings to transform my life and be present now, to live and tell this tale. Had I not learned from the dental experience, I might not have insisted on the removal of those moles until it was too late. The lesson strengthened me to fight for a life-or-death decision.

A large part of the process of finding oneself is finding presence. People have come into my life for a reason, a season, or a lifetime. The dentist and the doctor were there for a reason. Reasons and learnings can be both empowering and disempowering. Empowering moments touch one's heart and occur when presence exists within both parties. When this happens one remembers the place, time, and the feeling connected to the emotion which is connected to the learning, hence the memory. It is the connection of the feeling in a present moment in time that one remembers—the connection of the moments in life. As Cesare Pavese said, "We do not remember days, we remember moments."

Just like when two magnets attract and connect, connecting as one when in sync, it is in that absolute moment when connection occurs, where the magic happens and the lesson is learnt, when your needs are met by someone else's needs, and/or when their needs are being met by your needs. In every form of communication, there are two people's needs requiring to be met. When both are met, connection occurs. It is in this moment the magic is created and one remembers. The opposite also occurs, just like when two magnets repel and move in two different directions. When presence doesn't exist and when needs are not met, there is disconnect. When disconnect occurs, a disempowering learning is realized. Only if one is ready to search and recognize the learning, the situation can perhaps occur again until the learning is eventually acknowledged and learnt. One then becomes transformed.

Life for me was like a maze, turning here and there, working towards fulfilling outcomes and being suddenly faced with constant road blocks. I faced challenge upon challenge, dead ends in all I tried to achieve and do, obstacle upon obstacle. Life had changed and had become more difficult. Life was not supposed to be like this. It was not until, at a meditation retreat, I learnt life wasn't a maze at all; it was a labyrinth, a labyrinth being circular and only having one entrance and one exit. There is only one path into the depth of the circle of life, and we are navigating through the challenges, the trials and tribulations, and the learnings and transformations obtained from all the occurrences in life.

Remembering that everything happens for a reason, I ask myself, "What can I learn from this, and how can I use the learning moving forward into the next phase of the labyrinth and my life?" Each phase of life is one step closer to the exit. Upon physically exiting the labyrinth, which I walked around at the retreat, I experienced a connection with my creator and with all my loved ones who had passed over, a euphoric feeling of love and connection with those who are always with me in my life, whether physically or spiritually. It was like the scene in the Star Wars series, *Return of the Jedi*, at the end of the movie when Obi Wan Kenobi, Darth Vader, and Yoda all appear amidst the celebrations, connecting the light side with love and joy with a wonderful feeling of peace.

The meaning I took away from the labyrinth experience was, life is not as difficult and complicated as a maze; it is a simple labyrinth, one journey, one path, one entrance, one exit, all connected by love. Living through this epiphany was one of many, just like the chicken cracking open the eggshell and seeing the light for the first time with no way of returning back to the egg and forgetting the memory of the magnificent bright light it had experienced.

Life is simple and not complex! Life is not about overwhelm and anxiety. It is about focus and presence and the underlying factor of unconditional LOVE, first starting with self, to connect with others.

On my journey of life, my greatest mentor was my father: a solid, well-respected, intelligent, humble business man who provided for and protected his family. Unfortunately, he was also a man whose huge heart stopped beating far too early and did not meet any of his future generation.

Grandchildren today speak highly of him even though they never met him, a man they would choose to have dinner with over anybody else if they could only have that one opportunity, a man who left a legacy behind for them, a man we believe is looking down on us all, beaming with love and pride.

The greatest gifts he gave me were of confidence, a belief in self and a belief in hope, a strong rock-solid foundation of great values, including being honest, respectful, and good to people. He taught me to treat everybody equal no matter who they are and where they have come from. To this day, this mindset has given me the courage to communicate with a diverse range of people, people from different cultures, religions, and socioeconomic backgrounds from people on welfare, drug addicts, or street buskers to Chief Executive Officers and Prime Ministers. "No matter the differences, focus on the sameness. Treat all people with respect," he would say—great words of wisdom from my dad.

As the years passed by, the busyness within was becoming busier. The simple was becoming complicated, and the constant living and doing busyness was only becoming worse and showing up in my behaviour. At a time of weakness, a mentor whom I highly respect recognized the behaviour and told me, "It is not about working it all out. Stop doing and start being. Be, not Do.

Start with stop being hard on yourself. You are a valued person on the team." Wow! With her presence and with my presence along with the conciseness and preciseness of her message, I got it! The message was delivered. By her recognizing a pattern of behaviour in me, she called me on it and gave me the gift of awareness. I was open to her feedback, was honest with myself, and recognized the truth of how I was living my life. This happened at a time in my life when I did feel vulnerable and did not believe in myself. Perfect words, at a perfect time. Words I needed to hear. "Thank-you," I say to her.

I had been living in my head, and when you live in your head you're dead. Yes, that is where I was living from, my head, and I lost myself in the process. The deeper learnings I received from that one brief conversation were as simple as:

> Be not do.
>
> When being, I am present.
>
> When present, I am happy.

Presence is an actual lifetime present when one is present.

– Mia Tolis.

Establishing and recognizing the feeling of presence, at that moment, can be recalled when called upon. A university lecturer during my post graduate studies in counselling and a business associate come to mind when I recall "present people." I had heard about presence and thought I knew what it was and thought I was living it; however, I was not. Once I felt this feeling of presence when I myself was present, then I knew what it was. It was like, Lao Tzu's proverb:

"When the student is ready the teacher will appear. When the student is truly ready... The teacher will disappear."

I must have been ready for the gift of presence and, true to the proverb, both of these teachers have disappeared. I say thank you to these people for their lifelong gifts.

Being in the moment had a deeper meaning when I was in these people's presence. Concise, precise, direct communication introduced me to the concept of taking the emotion out and dealing with the facts, calling me out on truths and contextually expressing myself. Knowing when to speak and when to stay quiet and actively listen and be respectful when someone is speaking, to respond instead of reacting, to speak with kindness, honesty, and helpfulness, apologizing when only seeing a side from my perspective... These all taught me, when one behaves like this, the person is present. The presence, the moment, and recognizing two different perspectives when communicating is enlightening.

Often, when people only view from their own perspectives, they are present for themselves and not for the other person. The gift is when the Ah-ha moment is recognized and the person realizes it is from their perspective that they are communicating and not the person they are communicating with. The distinctions recognized in these transformations were quite extraordinary. Feelings and awakenings, which I call magic moments not to be forgotten and always to be remembered: these moments were quite extraordinary, just like the chicken being hatched from the egg. How had I lived my life? Where had I been? I must have still been living in the egg, or perhaps living inside my own bubble. These defining transformational moments led to my own awakening to life.

Presence is the most important factor when communicating; being there and listening are the basis of communication. Relationship building, both in business and in personal relationships, is about listening to one another's needs, moving in the same direction together, enabling mutual outcomes to be effectively achieved. When presence is not present, information can be misinterpreted, and unfortunately, outcomes become challenging to be fulfilled together. It becomes one long and painful journey through suffering to achieve outcomes. That is, if the outcomes are ever achieved. When presence is present and values are aligned, flow happens effortlessly, and everything seems to come together. When all is in flow, the magic happens.

The present of presence. For this I will be forever grateful. This is a further enlightening of the egg, a metaphor for my soul, allowing even more light to come in. It was whilst searching for presence in enlightened souls that the metaphor of "The Cappuccino" story came about. So, let me tell the story.

Throughout life, I would meet people and I would often notice, when communicating, only one person was connected to the conversation, and this was usually the speaker. Connection was only occurring on the surface level of the conversation. This surface level of the conversation is what I call the chocolate powder level as sprinkled on the milk froth of the cappuccino. This is noticed through body language, perhaps looking away, reactions to what is being said, and interpretations of what is being said. Often people are just being polite and eventually walk away. People just don't understand you, or perhaps you just don't understand them. It's like two people communicating in two different languages, communicating basically on two different wavelengths. You part ways, and life continues. It is my belief that people are just not present. Perhaps they are; however, by not understanding and not digging deeper and asking further questions, how will one understand what is being communicated? To be able to understand their world and what it is they are trying to communicate, comes down to the awareness of the presence, actively listening and being in the moment.

It is so easy to say "yeah, yeah" whilst nodding your head, conversing and pretending to listen when, in fact, one is zoning out and listening to one's own inner dialogue. Often one is too busy with concentrating on what is to be said next and does not capture and understand what is being said in the moment. At this level, there is a lot of noise and a lack of clarity and focus. Presence is missing, communication breaks down, and this is when misunderstandings occur.

The next level of depth in the cappuccino is the milk froth. The level of conversation and consciousness becomes a little deeper here, a little more presence, understanding, and a little more depth of the conversation occurring, including a more interested interaction between both parties. Through positive communication, connection and learnings are obtained.

Beneath the levels of chocolate powder and milk froth is the real depth and flavour of the coffee. Those present are searching for the elusive flavour and the elusive connection. Flavour, taste, and flow are found when focussing in the present moment. In the depths of the drinking glass, cup, or mug is where the smell, feel, and taste of the richness of the coffee is obtained—the essence of being present. It is in these depths where the magic of connection and communication happens, deep and meaningful conversations at a deeper level of consciousness. It is at this level that gems appear. Or, perhaps, one may call them gifts. These gifts are presents. Presents appear when there is presence.

Some people may not want to dig so deeply into the essence of life. One may be content living at the chocolate powder level or even choose to live at the milk froth level. There is no wrong or right level. It depends on one's own choices and where happiness lives for oneself. It also depends on one's own awareness of what one wants or needs. We are all different, just like all the choices of coffee one has. How do you like your coffee? Short black, long black, macchiato, flat white, café latte...as well as having it with or without sugar and whether milk is added, full cream milk, low fat, soy milk, almond milk, and the list goes on. It's your choice.

Chris, my husband, my greatest teacher, a good person, a noncomplicated person, is someone who appreciates just being and getting on with his life. Content is what I would now call him. However, it has not always been this way. He has been on his own journey and could be another chapter in this book, or perhaps a whole other book. I now understand: he is in my life so that he can show me the qualities I don't have or qualities I do have but may have forgotten about. He always sees the good in others, never a negative word or a judging word about others. Some even refer to him as Saint Christopher. Being with me for so many years, he too has transformed and continues to transform.

Chris came from a family completely opposite from my own. I came from a family of high achievers who were emotional, confident, strong, opinionated, and looking for inner happiness. Somehow, I married someone completely opposite to myself. The differences have often challenged us, and we continue to work through them, learning, growing, and transforming ourselves and each other and learning from one another. We continue to grow as individuals, enabling our marriage to grow to even higher and deeper levels, understanding and believing we all have what we need within us and have either relinquished or forgotten those qualities. These qualities are just lost until they are found again, and it is in the depths of one's greatest adversities that gems are found, otherwise known as lessons and learnings, and are often transformational.

As an adult returning to, once again, becoming an avid reader, I have discovered Elif Shafak's amazing novel, The Forty Rules of Love, based on the story of Rumi, the famous poet and mystic, and the teachings from his spiritual teacher, Shams of Tabriz, and it sums up our relationship and all relationships beautifully: "Every true love and friendship is a story of unexpected transformation. If we are the same person before and after we loved, that means we haven't loved enough." So very true. Lessons, learnings, and transformations are always taking place.

A belief running my thoughts, which I became aware of, was that everything in my world was about being right or wrong. Proving and making myself right and others wrong, being hard on myself and making myself wrong, also drove me to that "keep on doing" mentality. I needed to annihilate this right or wrong belief system. After all, I was an educator with over twenty years' experience, and the conditioning of correcting students' work had become a part of me. Letting go of this belief and the practice to do so took a lot of time and energy. However, the awareness and the freedom this gave me was enlightening in a sense that things just don't need to be right or wrong; they can just be. I sometimes notice that pattern of behaviour manages to still creep in. When I notice this, I ask myself, "In the scheme of things, is this really important?" And often, as I have now learnt, I shrug, nod my head, focus on my breath, and walk away, as often it is not.

A life-changing event was when the teacher became a student again, going back to university as a mature-aged student to study a post-graduate program in counselling and psychotherapy. This experience triggered a lot of my anxieties and beliefs, an absolutely wonderful life-changing event, including all the good experiences as well as all the challenging and stressful times. The awareness from all the gifts was transformational, just like a caterpillar when entering its chrysalis, never to be the same again and, upon exiting, transforming into a beautiful butterfly for the rest of its life.

Changing my mindset to transform my life was a process. In the past, I had not given myself permission to slow down and look after myself. My life was all for everybody else. Having travelled on this journey, I now give myself permission to care for myself. This is not being selfish. In the world of counselling, this is known as self-care. I have given a new empowering meaning to the word self-care. These days, I find myself asking a more empowering question. In the past, my subconscious inner dialogue would consistently ask, "What do I have to do next?" And, of course, I would go out looking for it. "Seek, and you shall find." These are powerful words one may have heard before from the Holy Book, and that is how I lived. Instead, I now say, "How can I appreciate even more the presence in this moment now?" Answering this question enables me to embrace and appreciate the moment with presence. Carpe Diem: seize the day/moment.

Transformational change is part of the healing process. We are all healing! Everyone has been hurt in one way, shape, or form. Part of our journey is to heal, and it is through transformational change that we get to where and what we want in life, leading to inner happiness.

Improving the practice of presence continues to be part of my process. It is a principle that continually requires to be practised. Meditation is the gym for the mind, just like a gym is for the body. Meditation builds muscle for the mind to help with focussing and staying present.

Meditation was a huge part of my transformation and healing process. Being in the moment—appreciating the simple things in life, having an attitude of gratitude, appreciating all the good in one's life—has helped in this journey of finding myself and inner happiness.

Commencing yoga and focussing on the breath supported me with becoming focussed and staying present. The poses performed in yoga class are all part of exercising the muscle of the mind. At the end of class, the Sanskrit word "Namaste" was said by the instructor and repeated by the yogis in the class. The meaning of the word Namaste is often interpreted as: "The light within me honours the light within you." During my third yoga class, I recognized that the word Namaste, in Greek, means "Just Be," an appropriate meaning and message, which resonates in a practice helping with healing and transforming in the present.

Attending the gym, yoga, and Pilates classes, with the occasional relaxation in the steam room and salt water hydrotherapy pool, all assisted in slowing down the mind and staying present.

As a five-year-old, I loved reading, so I returned to the world of reading novels. Reading greatly assisted me in staying focussed and present where I would lose myself amongst the pages within the confined world of the paperback.

I visit my gratitude journal every evening before I go to bed. Earlier I mentioned that I had been living in the world of scarcity. My journal has given me the gift of recognizing and remembering how much I really do have in my life, and it stems from having an attitude of gratitude. The most precious gift I am grateful for is the breath. We come into life with a breath and we leave life with a breath. The awareness of, the power of, and the presence of breath are powerful.

Recognizing that transformation has occurred and continues where supportive habits have been established makes life so much freer, happier, and relaxed. All I need to remember is that all I need is within me, and I am in control of my own thoughts, and lists do not control me.

Life now continues with the practice of exercising daily, whether walking, going to the gym, attending yoga or Pilates, meditating, or reading and journaling in my gratitude journal, all whilst being present! This is all I now need to find my inner happiness, which is as simple as focussing on one breath at a time and being present.

When living in the present, there is no anxiety or lists. Living a wonderful life from a beautiful present state where a grateful, happier person lives in a grateful, happier and peaceful place.

I once was lost and now I am found through simply being aware of the presents in the presence.

"Peace is all around us - in the world and in nature and within us in our bodies and our spirit. Once we learn to touch this peace, we will be healed and transformed.
It is not a matter of faith,
it is a matter of practice."

- Thich Nhat Hanh

"Our whole spiritual transformation brings us to the point where we realise that in our being, we are enough."

~ Ram Dass

CHAPTER SEVEN

Transitional Change

By Stephen R. Smith

My name is Stephen R. Smith. I currently live in Sarasota, Florida, USA. Originally from Canada, I've moved around from California, Washington State, Texas, and I now reside in Sarasota, Florida, which happens to be 'home of the number one beach in the USA'. The beautiful, white quartz sand beach is my favorite place to get grounded and, when I can, attend the Sunday evening Drum Circle, which is a spiritual experience that everyone should experience at least once in their life.

My transformational change has been a slow and not always steady process. It's been two steps forward and three steps back many times over the last 25 years. What I've realized is that I need to try again, fail again, try again, and fail better. If I don't like something, then I should change it. I have to change my perspective, my thinking, and my attitude toward whatever issue that I'm not feeling comfortable with. Some of these issues include feeling like I was not worthy, good enough, or smart enough to accomplish whatever I had set out to do. I had to rid myself of the self-hatred and self-loathing and the feeling that I wished I were dead, rather than continue to suffer and be a victim of my own creation so that I didn't have to feel this way anymore.

I have accomplished many wonderful things in my life: true, record-breaking achievements in my career, winning million-dollar government and public contracts, being awarded National Sales Manager of the Year, a first marriage that resulted in three amazing children, multiple houses, new cars, and a second marriage to a beautiful blonde trophy wife from Denmark. The fact was, I just didn't love myself and felt unworthy of everything that I had. I carried myself with a mask on: happy, successful, accomplished, and a feeling of authority, that I was better than the next guy. Others were simply inadequate when trying to measure up to me. "What a loser that person is", I would say to myself when I compared myself to others. Yet, here I was, just exactly that same person that I described them to be - no real positive asset to anyone, let alone the community at large - I was the kettle, calling it black and tarnished.

Currently, I am employed in a family business which I started in June of 2006, joined by my father, sister, brother, and another non-family member. We restore and refinish bathtubs, showers, tile, countertops, and sinks as a franchise, using an exclusive porcelain glaze that is safe and non-toxic. I love my job because I am able to utilize the artistic side of my personality by making old, worn out and dated things look like brand new. I'm able to transform things into a beautiful new state and give them new life. How's that for transformational change?

It is said that everything happens for a reason, but I don't necessarily believe that. I have to ask myself, "What role did I play in the outcomes that I experienced?" Too many times, I've had to learn the hard way, through trial and error. I made poor choices and didn't listen to good advise, and then had to experience the hard luck story, rather than apply the good suggestion I was given. I was the reason and the cause of my problems; although, I was told recently by a good friend that there are no problems in life, only issues that have yet to be resolved. Do I have to be hit by a car to learn that I should look both ways before I cross the street? No, I shouldn't have to use trial and error to see if that really happens, unless I have a death wish! I've learned that smart people learn from others' mistakes. A phrase by HP Technology rings in my head now, **"When everything else computes, the results are extraordinary"**.

My transformation didn't come to a higher perspective of life until I almost died in a car wreck and passengers got hurt because I was driving drunk. I happened to be living in El Dorado, California. Just five miles from Placerville, or better known as 'Old Hangtown'. Yes, it got this name from hanging people, mostly thieves back in the Gold Rush days, sometimes up to as many as 20 people at a time. It was only ten miles from Sutter's Mill, California, where gold was first discovered and caused the rush in 1849. I was there with my friends one fateful day, drinking and having a good old time. I got into an argument with my friend, whose house was across from the mill on the south fork of the American River. He was mad at me for making passes at his sister. Although she wasn't upset about it, he was. So, I got my buddies and jumped into my pristine 1986 Volare' RoadRunner and proceeded to speed out of town on a rainy night down the historic Highway 49. As I was coming around the corner at twice the posted 50 MPH speed limit, I slid off the opposite side of the road, broke off the power pole, flew through the air, and stopped dead when I hit an oak tree at about 20 feet off the ground and then dropped to earth with a giant thud. All I remember is the radio playing for a moment and then stopping; nothing but silence.

The next thing I knew, I was in the trauma unit at UC Davis Medical Center, which was 60 miles away, with a collapsed lung, severely fractured jaw, and a broken wrist. I ended up on the operating table for eight hours. I was told that they lost me a few times during the surgery to repair my jaw; a surgery that normally took two-three hours. I received blood transfusions, which, I believe ultimately led to my bout with hepatitis C some 17 years later. (This was before they were testing blood for communicable diseases like they do today.) I was in chemotherapy treatment for a year for hepatitis C, and I was ultimately cured of an 'incurable disease' at that time. I'll never forget the day that I got the news from my wife, the mother of my three children, whom sadly, I had recently separated from: the hospital needed me to come in immediately when I got back to Texas from my trip to California because they had detected the hepatitis C in a blood test that I had taken. I was visiting with my dear friend Steve, "Mr. Tub" - you'll hear more about how he has influenced me later in this story. When I heard the news, my initial thought was, 'that's it, I'm going to die soon, my life is over'; but it wasn't. By the grace of my higher power, whom I call God, I was spared.

I had been in the medical industry and toured the very first AIDS unit built in Seattle. I was on a sales call prior to their opening, and the Director of Nursing gave me the grand tour of this magnificent facility. It was adorned with apothecary bottles built into the pillars of the facility that they had excavated from the building site, which was originally a pharmacy. There was a blue room at the end of the hall at which point the Director of Nursing said to me, "This is the final stop. The patients can come down with diseases like hepatitis C, pneumonia and other illnesses and that will kill them." Apparently, that wasn't dramatic enough, and obviously, I wasn't grateful that I had survived a few near-death experiences to change my ways. Sure, I stopped drinking for years at a time, on several occasions. But I did what most alcoholics do, which was to fool myself with the belief that I could drink like other men. "I can handle this", I said to myself. Was I wrong? Absolutely. I was very wrong. I have yet to find any redeeming value that my drinking career has brought to me. On the other hand, it has brought much misery and loss in so many ways. But, where there is bad, there is also good. Equals and opposites, yin and yang, all part of the circle of life. It was really about perspectives.

I seemed to constantly get life to the point where it was really good, and then turn right around to tear it back down by making poor choices. My thinking, my beliefs, and my morals showed me how wrong I really was. I ended up divorced, then remarried to a beautiful Dane, whom I couldn't understand how I seemed to be so lucky as to have a wife like this; a blonde-haired, blue-eyed angel that was a former high fashion model in France. She even had her own clothing label and store at one time in Brentwood, California. Her clientele included the top stars in Hollywood. Ultimately, I moved with her from Texas to Florida to be closer to my mother and father, who lived in a penthouse on Siesta Key. I hadn't seen them much in years past, and this was an opportunity to go to greener pastures and be closer to them.

I had visited back in 1993, and knew that this was paradise, as I had never seen a beach like this before. I grew up on the West Coast in Southern California, and the beaches there were like gravel compared to the white, powder sand of Siesta Key. I had to leave my children behind in Texas with their mother, and this caused them to feel as if I had abandoned them. I allowed myself to lose touch with them and couldn't seem to put the money together to bring them to Siesta Key for at least a vacation in the summer. The worse I felt about this, the more distant I became. I had regrets over this for many years and it helped to firmly establish my disgust for myself. Remember now, I could wear that mask which said, "All is OK, I'm doing just fine". Little did I know (and would come to learn) that 'fine' can be the acronym for F'd up, Insecure, Neurotic and Emotional; hence, I became known as a deadbeat dad. Great huh? Life seemed pretty good on the surface, but alcohol was becoming a problem again. When I met my wife, I wasn't drinking at all, but she was. The time came when I finally threw in the towel and said to myself, "Well, if you can't beat them, join them", so I started drinking with her.

Our marriage lasted only four years. Together, my new wife and I drank ourselves apart, and I ended up divorced for the second time. By this time, I really hated myself for destroying two marriages and I certainly felt sorry for myself and had run out of self-esteem. I was lost and didn't know what to do. I had ended my relationship with my second wife when I went to jail for a domestic loss of control (on my part) and a fit of anger over a door being left wide open as she was complaining to me about something. Only God remembers what she was saying, I surely don't. Down and out of jail, she had left me. The only reason I had any personal possessions at all was because my parents had picked up my things.

While I was in jail, my bunk mate and I became fast friends. He was a tree climber and knew the tree business. So, I talked with my father and he bought the things we needed to open a tree-trimming company. Fabulous! I knew about chainsaws and had used them since I was a teenager. This seemed like a natural choice for a business. Don't tell me money doesn't grow on trees because it does...when you trim them. What I didn't realize at the time was that I had surrounded myself with people who were not making healthy choices. I had a few more near-death experiences, came close to having the staff drop trees on customers' houses, had two of my crew almost kill themselves because they were not fit to have a chainsaw in their possession, and it was my fault because I was not paying close enough attention to their abilities. My car was on its last legs. (The Buick wasn't a truck, but I was treating it like one, and it eventually just gave out on me.) I prayed to God for things to change - for a new opportunity. I decided to close the business because I had to do something different. God answered my prayer.

I was reading the newspaper and I viewed a 'Help Wanted' ad for a Bathtub Refinisher. I said to myself, "I can do this", even though I had never refinished a tub before. This is where my friend Steve comes back into the story. I was his assistant back in 1983 when he had started his own tub refinishing franchise. I've known this man since my freshman year in High School, back in 1975 at Mission Viejo High School. I had a basic understanding of what this was all about, that's for sure. I called the number listed in the ad and spoke with the owner. I explained my circumstances about how I desired a change in my career and told him I knew about this industry. To my amazement, he hired me on my first call to him. I ended up buying the equipment needed to do this job (on payments of course); I even bought the truck from one of his employees to get into business as an Independent Technician on behalf of their company.

I worked for this company for a little over a year. Around the same time, I met a girl who was very spiritual. She even attended a church called The Center of Spiritual Awareness. Led by Reverend Duffy, this is where I made a huge spiritual transition. I owe much of my growth to these two ladies. I learned about The Law of Attraction, and I moved from a place of being an average, typical Christian to a higher plane of Self: 'I Am'. I became enlightened to the power of the Christ Consciousness, and came to believe that the Universe supports me in whatever I choose. I learned that thought is creative and that God is the original causation. I started to actually love myself and began the process of healing from my past and being grateful; and most importantly, I was learning to be present in any given moment.

As I mentioned before, transformational change is a slow process and I had to go backwards again several times before I could continue to move forward. I'd have times of pretty smooth sailing, and times of pure hell, particularly when I decided to take back control of my life from God. I was overly confident and too comfortable, which resulted in much suffering for me and those around me.

The definition of insanity is doing the same thing over and over again and expecting a different result. I did this for most of my life. I didn't take the sound advise from my family and friends; rather, I had to do it for myself, and in the end, I always ended up having to say, "You were right and I was wrong". One of the most profound experiences I had was being exposed to Cognitive Behavioral Therapy. I had to go through a process of addressing my belief systems and recognizing that most of what I thought to be true actually wasn't.

I feel that my parents did a good job of teaching me to be honest, hard-working, considerate, dedicated, loyal, and have proper social manners. I don't know exactly where and when I veered down the wrong path, but I'm pretty certain it had to do with using drugs and alcohol at a young age and not learning the proper emotional coping skills. I had to learn this later in life - to build a tool box of answers to combat my demons. I also had to retrain my thinking to one of positivity, as well as change some of my core values. It is a continuing process every day to keep myself on track, and I know that in the flicker of a moment, if I am not careful, total deterioration of everything good can be wrecked rather quickly.

An example of this occurred back in 2010 when I made the choice to drink and drive and wrecked my sister's Lexus. Little did I realize the severity of my decision. I ended up in jail for over seven months, lost everything that I had built up, bought, and owned, and I caused extreme grief for my family and friends. What a sorry state of affairs I had created. I ended up homeless, living in the woods. I am not looking for sympathy. Oh, no…I deserved the consequences of my actions for sure.

Today, I love myself. I look in the mirror, smile, and tell myself, "You're Okay!" I accept me for who and what I am.

I found my purpose, and every day I work at achieving my dreams and goals. They are to improve myself and to make me a better, more productive individual. It takes hard work, dedication, consistency, discipline, and the knowledge and faith that I can be successful and stay on the right path. I do it one day at a time. I had to fall down many times to get where I am today. A saying I like is "Try again, fail again, try again, fail better." I simply get back up whenever I fall down. I try to learn from my mistakes, but even better, I learn from the mistakes of others so as not to make the same mistakes myself. I get better because I don't give up. I can have anything I want. It starts with a thought. Then, I claim that thought, make an action plan, and aspire to achieve that goal.

I have a higher power that I call God. Jesus is my Savior, and when I turn over my life and my will to them, things start to change for the better. I accept life on life's terms, rather than trying to be the one in charge and the chief critic. I start my day early, at three or four o'clock in the morning. The first thing I do is listen to motivational videos to establish a positive thinking mode and attitude which helps guide me to become a better person. I want to inspire others to count their blessings and to pay it forward. I realized that I had to eliminate incorrect and limiting beliefs and replace them with new positive thinking, which enables me to be a productive, reliable contribution to my children, my family, my friends, and the community that I live in. I try to live each day like it's my last day on Earth. I cannot change the past, it's just memories; it is gone. Every day that I wake up breathing, it's brand new, and I can paint the canvas of it any way that I choose. I may have the future if I live past today; all I really have is the present moment. It's called that, because it's a gift.

"And even though the healing hurt, she couldn't help but marvel at the beauty of her own transformation"

~ Rebecca Ray

CHAPTER EIGHT

Heal Your SoulSelf

By Kim Joss

Four years ago, I awoke from a nap, realizing that I had missed a call I had been expecting, a call that would determine my health, my treatment plan moving forward, and my future. There were so many tests, procedures, and lots of waiting and wondering to get to this point. It was an extremely stressful and emotionally draining time for me and my family.

I took a deep breath and retrieved the voicemail. My eyes began to well up as I listened to the message: "You need to come into the office." In that moment, I just knew. By this time, the tears were flowing down my face as I walked upstairs to deliver the news to my husband, Eric. He knew immediately that I did not get the news we had been hoping to hear. I knelt on the bed and told him that I needed to make an appointment and go into the office. He always kept me grounded and calm, and he knew the right things to say to make me feel better. We agreed: it is what it is. We would get through this. Everything happens for a reason, and the reason was not clear and was confusing at that moment.

No matter how positive my attitude and thoughts were, my health had been compromised. IT was already inside of me, growing and about to change my life. I did not want to die. I did not want this to be the end. I had a lot of life to live and experience. I was not ready to leave this earth or my family. I wanted to be around to watch my girls grow up and to be a part of their celebrations of life. That was my motivation and drive to do whatever it would take. It was ready to go to war with me, and I was prepared to fight.

I never imagined at the age of 37 that I would hear the C word being tossed around. I did not feel sick. I did not have any signs or symptoms. I thought I was healthy. I mean I was eating right, taking care of my body, making healthy choices, working out and training for a fitness competition. How could I be sick? How could this be happening? Why was this happening? All these thoughts were swirling through my head and weighing on my mind.

A couple of years before this happened, I was on the path to reclaiming my health, a decision I'd made after the day I realized I had hit my highest weight to date and I was tired after just walking up the stairs at the age of 35. I mean, what was 45, 55, 65 going to look and feel like? I had fallen into that parent persona and lost my identity. I figured, I'm a parent; this is how it's supposed to be. You let yourself go; you stop taking care of yourself. I did not want to be that parent or person anymore. I could be a good mom and wife and a better role model to my girls by being healthy, fit, comfortable and confident and still have my own identity. I found this served myself, my girls, and our family much better.

Changing my lifestyle literally saved my life. One day I came home from the gym, took off my sweaty sports bra, laid on the floor in an awkward position, reached across my side for an itch, and I felt something. It was a lump or a bump of some sort. It felt odd, but I didn't think much of it. Until the following week at Thanksgiving, when I found out my sister had had a scare, so I asked her to feel it, and she was insistent that I get it checked out immediately. And she followed up with me to be sure I made an appointment. I wasn't that person who went to the doctor for everything. You know, you get busy and put yourself off. Well, that had changed now. I quickly learned that I needed to make myself a priority and listen to my body.

And you know what? If it hadn't been for that millisecond when I felt that 1.5-cm tumor that would change my life, and if I had not gone to the doctor to get it checked out, or if I had not started on my path to get healthy, I would not be here today. That is powerful and scary at the same time.

On the day of surgery to remove the breast cancer, my family and friends packed the waiting room. I was surrounded by so much love and support. I truly had amazing people in my life that would drop or rearrange everything to be there for me and lift me up in love and prayers. They were there for me even if it was just to squeeze my hand as the nurses placed the IVs, to make me laugh to keep my mind off of it all, to wipe my tears and tell me everything would be okay, and to offer the hugs, kisses, and I-love-you's as they wheeled me away for my prep procedures or surgery.

I felt a sense of relief removing the beast from my body, and now we would wait to see what the pathology report revealed. I feel like the waiting and wondering was almost the hardest part. That feeling of the unknown. It can really play some mean tricks with your mind if you let it. I did my best to not let it, but sometimes it did get the best of me. Oftentimes I would need to check my thoughts and reframe the circumstances. I found that my weaknesses were molding into strengths during it all. It helped me grow stronger. After all, you don't go through things; you grow through things.

The pathology report was back, and the news drastically changed the treatment plan. It was stage one, with a grade two to three, which meant it was very aggressive and, to top it off, it was HER2/neu. My oncologist explained that it did not need a host and it did what and how it wanted to do. The treatment plan went from surgery to remove the tumor, radiation, and five years of medicine to a year of chemotherapy with infusions every three weeks, a shot for my immune system each day afterwards, radiation, and oral medicine for five to ten years. Since I would be having so many infusions and blood draws and I was terrified of needles, installing a port in my chest was suggested and agreed upon. It took some time to process the delivery of this new information and treatment plan. We moved forward.

Our girls knew what I was going through. We needed to sit them down and let them know that things would be changing quite a bit in my treatment plan, how things might be different around the house with me, and how it would affect all of us. We didn't know how my body would react to the infusions; we needed to go with the flow and address things as they happened. Inevitably, I would eventually lose my hair.

I was determined to stay strong and not let the cancer own me. It was a battle. Sometimes I won and sometimes I surrendered. I always reminded myself that I am alive; I get a second chance and there are others who do not get that opportunity, or they have more invasive treatment plans than I had. I kept my heart grateful and focused on the positive. That is where I put my attention and thoughts.

I was known as the holiday healthcare patient. My first surgery fell on Valentine's Day, and the second fell on St Patrick's Day. It was time for my first infusion. I did not know what to expect. It hit me pretty hard. I became so sick. I had several side effects. I became dehydrated, which landed me in the hospital to pump fluids through my body. I used to drink a gallon of water a day, and now the scent and taste of it was extremely hard for me to tolerate. All my senses—sound, sight, smell—had become heightened. My family would joke with me that I had super Spidey senses. At times they worked in my favor; other times, they were a struggle.

It is hard to put into words how I felt. The best way to describe it is the flu times 1000. I was exhausted and weak most of the time. The symptoms and side effects I was experiencing led me to be on several prescriptions. I am not an advocate for big pharma and masking the real problem, but sometimes you just give in and accept that there is a time and place for medicine and welcome it with open arms to manage and feel better.

I was pretty confident that I could continue my daily activities. That was not always the outcome. I continued working full-plus-time, which I believe helped to keep me busy and to keep my mind off of everything. If I felt good, I went for a walk, to the gym, got together with friends, ate well…but most times I felt miserable, resting and sleeping on the couch. And thinking. That was the most frightening. It was almost too much. You drive yourself into a state of mind, like…Why did this happen? What caused it? How did I get cancer?

We had changed our lifestyle and were a healthy family. We were GMO-free and organic. We spent a great deal of time researching ingredients and were the ones in the grocery store for hours reading labels. It was an adjustment. Our health was worth it. Our bodies are a gift. We only get one, so we definitely needed to honor it and treat it like the blessing it was. I also started becoming aware that it's not only what you put into your body, but also on your body, what you're breathing, what you're thinking and saying to yourself, the environment you choose to immerse yourself in. I do know one thing. Before I was diagnosed, I was a worrier. I was stressed. That does not serve you or your health well. I let go of things that did not matter. I used to worry and stress about little things, and they weren't the big things. So, I let it go. I found peace in being free from those feelings, and it improved my way of life and the lives of those around me.

Ironically, I should have been more stressed and worried. We hit rock bottom. The company Eric had been employed with for 15 years shut down leaving him laid off for several seasons. The owner decided unexpectedly to retire two years earlier than planned. We had intended on investing and turning it into our own future business; unfortunately, that did not come to fruition. Everything happens for a reason. It was a blessing in disguise that we did not put all our savings into the business buyout, because we would not have had insurance for two months, and that is when I was diagnosed. To top it off, the company I had been employed with for a very short amount of time was taken over by new management, not understanding at all about my circumstances or situation. Eventually, I was let go. I'd signed a sales agreement that stated, if I was not performing there would be a two-week turnaround, and if things had not improved, I would be let go. At the time, I did not think anything about not being able to perform due to medical reasons. I am fully aware for future endeavors and have preached to others about a medical clause.

You know that saying: you could be killing it at a job that would replace you in a week if you dropped dead. It's absolutely true. Not all employment establishments care about their employees and their previous work ethics.

I was partnered with a direct sales company in the 12 years prior, and with our healthy lifestyle changes, my passion changed and my heart left. I was never going to do anything like this again. I was just going to get that job. I did get that job. It served its purpose for the time. Although I could not help but feel I was trading time for money, I was working full-plus-time on some else's visions and dreams so that they could live their lifestyle. I didn't love what I was doing; it did not bring me joy. I wasn't excited or passionate to do what provided a paycheck. I wanted more and felt I was meant for something more. Before our unforeseen circumstances, we were comfortable yet settling. I wasn't truly happy with what I was doing. I did not just want to create a living; I wanted to create a life I absolutely loved and was passionate about.

You know, the one where you wake up excited to go to work. I knew there was something more for me.

I finally said yes to partnering with another organization when my health was compromised. I was so desperate for nutrition and hydration while going through my treatments. I knew I needed to take back control my health and life; yet I could not go back to doing it the way I did it before. I was exhausted and not seeing the results from all the hard work I was putting in. It was not maintainable or sustainable. I needed to work smarter, not harder. Not focus on the scale or a size, but on true whole-body health solutions. The treatments left my body worn out. I wasn't eating or drinking enough. I had stopped working out. My body responded to the treatments by blowing up like a balloon. It was threatened, and it was protecting itself. I had a closet full of smaller-sized clothes from my previous transformation, lots of clothes that no longer fit. I felt like a sausage trying to fit into my clothes. I was so hard on myself—emotionally abusive, to be exact. I finally came to the conclusion that I was here—right now. I would get to where I wanted to be, but for now I needed to feel comfortable and be gentle on myself after everything I'd gone through. I decided it was best to purchase some clothes that would fit me for the time being while working towards where I wanted to be.

While I was fighting for my life, my sister was bringing new life into the world. We joked about my nephew and I racing to see whose hair would grow the fastest. Yes, the time came, after cutting my hair shorter and shorter, one day in the shower it was coming out in clumps and it was so itchy that I had to make the appointment to shave my head and pick up the two wigs I had selected.

I would walk past the mirrors in our home and wonder who was this person staring back at me. For my sanity, I actually removed the one that I had to pass by multiple times a day. My life had been completely turned upside down.

Once I rang that victory bell at the cancer center, it was a celebration. Except I was left lost and broken. It had taken so much from me. Even though I tried to not let it, it did. With some things, I did not have a choice; I simply had to accept. Some things I did accept, and I grew and become stronger from them. Regardless, so much of my life was affected and changed. I needed to focus on adjusting, redirecting, and healing. After you ring that bell, you are free, and you've won the fight. Yet you are left to pick up the pieces and figure out what's next, how to move forward and let go of this part of your life that has consumed you for so long. I had to recreate and reinvent myself from the inside out. I understood and accepted that I would never be the same person I used to be. I made the choice to embrace it. But I still questioned it, cursed it, cried about it, and prayed about it. I wasn't in a good place. I was being extremely hard on myself. I was emotionally abusive to myself. My girls would see and hear me say not-so-nice things to myself. It was not healthy, and I was not being a good role model for my children. Health is not just what you're eating, but what you're saying, thinking, and believing.

No matter how positive or strong you are, you still have to deal and process. It finally sunk in and hit me like a brick wall. I fell into a dark place of depression and seclusion. I cut myself off from the world. I was present in what needed to be done, with the support of my family. Eric had stepped up big time. He took over most of the household duties: the laundry, cooking, cleaning, shopping, running the kids around. We had some wonderful friends that helped out with the kids' activities and whatnot when Eric went back to work or had a job pop up here and there.

I sort of went MIA and shut out the world and the people in it. I came across a grief cycle that explained what I was going through. It went: shock, numbness, denial, emotional outbursts, anger, fear, searchings, disorganization, panic, guilt, loneliness, isolation, depression, re-entry troubles, new relationships, new patterns, hope, affirmation, helping others. I experienced it all.

The biggest challenge for me was that re-entry: how to enter the social world again. I was prescribed Ativan to help me through the treatments. I no longer wanted to cover up and mask what I was going through. I wanted to deal, process, and heal. I had some odd things happening emotionally and physically. I trusted a holistic doctor and naturopath to help me uncover what was happening. I was off, not in balance; something was not right. After several tests, we discovered that I had an autoimmune disease, hypothyroidism, estrogen dominance, multiple vitamin and mineral deficiencies, high cortisol levels, adrenal fatigue, severe sensitivity and almost allergy to eggs and dairy. Once I incorporated the natural recommendations and eliminated the causing sources, my body became balanced and aligned, and I was feeling so much better overall. After much research, I decided to implement a plant-based vegan diet as well.

The most courageous thing you will do is let go of the version of yourself that no longer serves you. We are not perfect human beings, nor do we have to pretend to be, but it is necessary for us to be the best version of ourselves that we can be.

What was it that made me change? What was it that got me off the couch and doing things I enjoyed again? It wasn't just one thing that clicked and made everything clear. It was a lot of little changes, which added up to big things, that created the shift in me. I was given a second chance at life. It was a gift, and I needed to start acting like it.

My goal was to become a vibrant, healthy, fully engaged human, because that's the kind of person who loves well and serves well.

I began the healing process. I began to practice self-love. I began loving myself healthy. I began to experience joy. I began being raw, real, authentic, and vulnerable in what I speak and share. I recreated, reinvented, and allowed my soul to shine bright.

I began to be devoted to self-care and loving myself more. Loving yourself is the art of unconditional self-acceptance, self-respect, and positive self-image. I began saying kind things to myself, along with what I loved and appreciated about myself. I started doing nice things for myself and things that I truly enjoyed. To some this might seem selfish, but it's not. You have to take care of yourself before you can take care of others.

I intentionally set some personal guidelines and rules for myself as I started my journey to whole body health, wellness, and well-being.

I practiced being ever so kind to my whole body, health, and well-being.

I practiced being genuinely happy with working smarter not harder.

I practiced focusing on balance and moderation instead of restrictions and limitations.

I practiced on committing to a 90% nutrition and 10% fitness lifestyle.

I practiced making exercise a celebration of what my body can do and not a punishment for what I eat.

Setting these guidelines and having no expectations had me glowing from the inside out, experiencing joy, and feeling comfortable and confident.

I tried new types of being fit while making it fun. I was invited to start trail riding with my brother-in-law. It seemed like an adventurous way to get back into a fitness regime. The different trails and routes were exciting. The longer rides challenged me in a positive manner.

I found my passion and love for yoga. I love taking the time to honor and appreciate my body, mind and spirit to meditate, to think, and just be one with my body: bringing peace to my body and mind by quieting the chaos and noise of the world and all that's racing around me.

My journey has attracted the right kind of people into my life. I look back and I am humbled and grateful for all the genuine souls that were sent to me either to serve as a lesson or blessing, or both.

We were at rock bottom, both unemployed. Our saving accounts, emergency reserves, and backup funds were dwindling, then empty. We sold things, including our car. The medical and job-loss debt was multiplying at a very fast rate.

I am ever so grateful for being open to new opportunities and possibilities and aligning with my new lifestyle and amazingly generous organization that introduced me to residual income and time freedom. If it hadn't been for this opportunity, we would never have made it through financially. Now I wake up every day excited and passionate to coach, mentor, empower, and inspire others on their journeys. I experience pure joy in being able to serve and give back in so many ways to so many different people. I have met and surrounded myself with like-minded people that I am humbled to call my friends. We are all on our separate journeys, yet have a desire for health, happiness, healing, and to live our big best lives.

I now realize all of this did not happen to us; it happened for us.

After all, I couldn't just settle for anything; my daughters are watching.

I wanted them to see, know, and recognize.

It's okay...

to not be okay;

to be scared;

to be different;

to be strong;

to be uncertain;

to be fearless;

to be vulnerable;

to be weak.

And it's necessary...

to make themselves a priority;

to be their authentic selves;

to change, grow, and learn;

to not care what anyone thinks;

to challenge themselves;

to be kind to others;

to give, love, and serve;

to live unapologetically.

"I have traveled through madness to find me."
-Danny Alexander

It has taken over three years of growth, personal investment and development, standing stronger and prouder, digging deeper, loving myself harder, and owning every bit of it to get to this place with my beautiful awakened soul.

I will never be the same, and you know what? I am so okay with that, because I fucking love the new me. And I'm just getting started.

I am whole. I am free. I am an even better being because of the storms that I have endured which led me on my journey.

Don't let my words fool you. I'm not perfect and don't want to be. This version of me wasn't built overnight. This is experience. This is pain. This is struggle. This is insecurities.

This is abuse. This is challenges. This is depression. I had to go through all of these things to get to the level I'm at now.

I want to inspire and impact others to take back control of their health and lives. I want to show them how to be proactive and preventative with their whole-body health and well-being.

I want to help women and men to find their identities, their voices, their power, their peace within themselves. I want to build belief, breathe hope, inspire, empower, encourage, and challenge you to go deep, to find you, be you, love you. And to never give in or give up.

Everything is inside you. It's time to let the love and healing begin.

"You cannot heal what you don't reveal."
-Jay Z.

Awaken your soul. Awaken yourself. Allow your soulself to feel the energies. It will be profound, powerful. Let it surface, let it in. It will be uncomfortable at times. Your emotions will arise and flow. Let them. Tap into your authentic power. Spend some time sifting through your thoughts, feelings, and blocks. Then forgive, let go and free yourself so you can Heal Your SoulSelf.

"The only way to make sense out of change is to plunge into it, move with it, and join the dance."
~ Alan W. Watts

CHAPTER NINE

Transformation

By Elli Petrovska

Throughout your life there are many phases when you "want to" and "try to" re-invent yourself for a fresh new beginning. Whether the reason is to escape a situation or to better yourself, in these moments when we are alive, we feel full of energy, optimism and drive. Like so many, I have also said "I should", "I must", "I want to", "One day", and like so many, that day never arrived for the numerous ideas and plans that I slowly buried as if they never existed. The problem is that they are never laid to rest; they exist somewhere in the back of our minds and come to haunt us, the all too painful regrets of what could have been, only if.

Somewhere between the heightened state of "wow" and the death of these ideas and plans, we find that the state of fear, self-doubt and negative self-talk takes over. Sometimes we are aware of these feelings that overcome us like a toxic, unwanted guest, but most times we are unconscious to them until it's too late - until we look back and learn a valuable lesson. I've always wondered why some ideas come to life just as I planned them, and then so many others are long forgotten, and some never stood a chance as the familiar, dark self-imposed thoughts make themselves right at home.

We are all, on some level, afraid of change...afraid of failing and being judged by our family, friends, colleagues and community. As strange as it may sound, sometimes we are even afraid of the changes that success will bring. Think about that: if you were to be successful, you automatically think of the gains, whether they be of a financial nature, status, new friends or other benefits. The other side of success, which is somewhat in the back of our minds like a quiet whisper, yet detrimental to the outcome, is the thought of our losses after the success. The biggest loss is the thought of the people we may lose in the process of achieving success. We think that our nearest and dearest will be there to support us; however, we know that this is not always true. We all know someone who has succeeded, and the cost of that success is the loss or breakdown of their families or closest relationships.

The very thought of change can terrify us into a state of total inaction. It is easier to remain the same - not having to take action, not having to worry about achieving, not being judged, taking no risk, not experiencing any further losses. But do we really know the real cost of remaining the same? Have we really asked ourselves and thought about what is the ultimate long-term cost to our health, our relationships, our well-being? What is the real cost we pay with our lives for every dream we bury one by one just because we are afraid of change, afraid of losses, afraid of judgements? You have to question the fear, be it fear of losses, judgements or just change...is it just an illusion?

I have experienced that the 'fear of change' has no discrimination in relation to our current state of well-being, whether we are happy or miserable in our lives. If we are currently comfortable in our lives, even though we know the benefits of all the gains, we can still be paralysed with the fear of change because we have the illusion of some form of potential loss that may or may not ever happen. On the flip side, if we are not happy in our lives, and we may be in some form of pain, discomfort or we are just not content, the fear of change is still as strong and paralysing for the same reason. Even though we know that we would be better off by changing, the illusion of some form of losses overtakes us and stops us from moving forward.

The reality is that there will be gains and losses whether we change or not; that's just life! We must experience change. Just as the seasons change, so do phases in life. But it is never the end until your last breath. I have found that there will be mountains to climb, there will be decisions to make at crossroads, there will be obstacles along the road, and sometimes, we will need to take a detour. There will be times when you're swimming upstream against the flow and you have to turn yourself around to find your flow. There will be times when it feels like you're stuck on a mountain, looking up at an avalanche coming towards you and a tsunami coming at you. Sometimes, you just take each month or each week as they come, and in other times, you will work just to survive each day.

When you remain the same, you continue to carry the same beliefs, the same values, the same knowledge, the same fears and the same negative self-talk. To understand the underlying hidden costs of remaining the same, regardless of your age, you need to ask yourself, "How will I be throughout the rest of my life if I decide to remain the same by carrying all this baggage?"

Imagine staying the same, whether it be for the next five years or 50 years. How will your life turn out? To help you try to understand the real cost paid in life for staying the same, try thinking about your biggest goal that you are either stuck on or have not started. What is the biggest goal at the top of your list? (Either a real list or one that's just in your head.) Once you've identified the goal, if it's easier for you, feel free to ask a friend to help facilitate the questions in the exercise below:

When you are ready, focus on this one goal and imagine how your life turns out over the next five years in the scenario where you *did not* change. Because you did not change imagine carrying the same beliefs, the same values, the same knowledge, the same fears and the same negative self-talk. To really feel the downstream impacts to your life because you did not change ask yourself the below main questions then the sub-questions. More importantly feel your answers physically, mentally and emotionally, and visualise your life over the next five years.

- **How will you be better off and more successful in five years?** Does this make you happy? How does this make you feel? Was it worth staying the same?

- **Will you be content?** Does this make you happy? How does this make you feel? Was it worth staying the same?

- **What are you still fearing?** Is this fear valid? Does this make you happy? How does this make you feel? Was it worth staying the same?

- **What is the impact to your family relationships?** Who is still around? Who is no longer around? Does this make you happy? How does this make you feel? Was it worth staying the same?

- **What is the impact to your friendships?** Who is still around? Who is no longer around? Does this make you happy? How does this make you feel? Was it worth staying the same?

- **What is the impact to other relationships?** How will you treat them? How will they treat you? Will they tolerate you? Does this make you happy? How does this make you feel? Was it worth staying the same?

- **What is the impact to your health?** Will you be healthier? Does this make you happy? How does this make you feel? Was it worth staying the same?

- **What is the impact to your character?** Will you be nicer? Will you be more charitable? Will you be respected? Will you become bitter? Does this make you happy? How does this make you feel? Was it worth staying the same?

- **What do you look like?** Does this make you happy? How does this make you feel? Was it worth staying the same?

Now repeat these questions and imagine your life in another ten years, and then keep repeating until your aged around 100. Keep imagining and feeling your what your future life will be like, as if your actually living it. Feel your answers visually, emotionally and physically.

Once you have asked yourself these questions and visually imagined your life and felt it emotionally and physically, then there's only one more question to ask yourself to move forward. That question is, "Can I continue to live like this?" I'm guessing your answer will be "No"; in fact, if this goal is at the top of your list of goals, then the answer should be a big, fat "Hell no!"

We all know that change is inevitable, whether we control it or not. We have all experienced change in some form, be it good or bad. We also know that loss is inevitable too, whether we control it or not. So why do we self-sabotage? Some common beliefs and reasons we somehow manage to convince ourselves are; that we don't have the time, we don't have the money, we don't have the contacts, or even worse, our family and friends will think we're just plain crazy.

What we don't always do is question ourselves. We don't try to find a workaround, a way to make it work. In the instance of the most common illusion that we don't have enough time, do we even understand how we manage our time? Even more so, do we even understand that our concept of time depends on what we are doing? Isn't it strange how time goes so fast when we are in a state of high motivation or doing something that we love? In this state we forget to track time and it just flies, as the common saying goes. On the other side, when we are in a state of boredom or doing something that we are not happy doing or with people that we don't like, the time passes so painfully slowly, yet the definition of time, "24 hours a day", remains the same.

It is our perception of time based on what we are doing that drives our need to learn how to better to manage our time. Question everything that you are prioritizing time for in your life. Before you make time for it, ask yourself, "Does this add value to my life?" If it does add value and there is a benefit for you or someone else, then make time. If it's something that you must do, then just schedule it in and do it. Regardless of the action, always ask yourself, "What value does this add to my life?" and "How can I do it better?"

Then the biggest killer of time that is just as bad as our fears, that stops us from taking action to move forward, is time wasted on non-value-add activities, people and events. This can be as simple as watching TV or socialising with people that drain our energy. We all are guilty of this; it's one of the biggest lessons we learn in life. Time is so precious and we cannot get it back, so be wise on how you spend your time by making it a priority to spend it with people and things that bring value as opposed to draining you.

The other big belief that stops us from moving forward is the illusion of 'I don't have the money'. I'm not saying this is an easy fix, but have you really explored all your options? For example, there are government grants for new businesses, just speak to your accountant! For extra savings, have you asked if you can work extra hours? For bigger investments, have you spoken with your bank or broker to inquire if you can take out a loan? If not, perhaps you can find a joint venture money partner?

Another way we can get stuck or held back from taking action is by heeding advice from our family, friends and colleagues - the people we care for. Often times, what we fail to ask ourselves is what their level of expertise is on the matter. Have the people who are giving this advice 'been there done that'? Have these people succeeded as credible role models that are worthy of following? Have these people made the money that you want to make? For example, if I want to be a billionaire, should I ask for advice from someone who is not even a millionaire? Of course not! You need to find the right people with the right mindset before asking for guidance on how to approach your specific goal, be it in person or online. Instead of giving up, try networking with people you know or start meeting new people. Attend seminars of interest and relevance to your goal so that you can network. This is also an education opportunity, whether it be a free event or not.

The message here is to keep trying until you've exhausted all possible options as to which solutions will work, and which will not work for your individual situation. Always look for a better, more efficient way to take action. Save time and energy to work smarter, not just harder. When you're not getting the results you're after, ask yourself, "What am I doing right?", and "What am I doing wrong?" Have you tried a different solution?

Albert Einstein quoted **"The definition of insanity is repeating the same behaviours and expecting a different outcome".** We are all guilty of unconsciously thinking that our same beliefs and mindsets can get us through any life situation; after all, it is easier to remain in our comfort zones. To experience transformation in our lives, we need a different way of thinking, a different state of awareness in relation to our beliefs, our self-value, and our fears. To change, we need self-awareness; and we need to not only acknowledge our fears, we need to feel them and deal with them to be able to let go of them so they do not paralyse us. We cannot learn and develop and just go back to being the same and doing the same because we will not get a different result.

So now what? How do we bring on change, manage that change, and transform our lives with successful outcomes? From life experience through trial and error and self-reflection, I have found that there are **three key factors** to form a solid platform for achieving success in life:

> 1. Through life experience ups and downs, we need to **learn the lessons** that life is trying to teach us.
>
> 2. Know yourself by understanding who you are and who you're not, and more importantly, **develop self-value**.
>
> 3. **Make a decision and take action,** which achieve the results that meet your goals and purpose.

Each of the sections below describe in more detail how you can lay the foundations for real transformation in your life, regardless of where you are tracking in life now. At any time, you can review your life lessons, re-assess your self-value and make new decisions to drive you to take action to achieve high-value results and success.

Learn the Lessons

During this journey called "life", from the beginning and right til the end, we will experience events that will mould us and change us, sometimes to stay on the same road and sometimes to completely change course. People will come and go; sometimes they'll come back and sometimes they won't. Either way, it will be ok, and as the saying goes, "This too shall pass". Just like the seasons, it's never the end of the world, even if it feels like it at the time. We have to accept that it just *is;* we need to feel the pain, feel the joy, and feel the moment. We cannot change the past but we can surely learn from it. We cannot guarantee the future, we can only hope. What's left is the "now" or "living in the moment".

I have learned many lessons in life so far; however, the three biggest lessons that stand out (and are the most painful lessons learned) are the following: there is no such thing as 'forever', there is only now. No amount of promises can guarantee the so called 'forever'. The other lesson is that there is no such thing as perfect, and let me tell you that this is coming from a so-called perfectionist. I have learned we can always improve, regardless of where we are, we are always learning and we always have the opportunity to be better.

As time goes on, not only do our lives change, our cultural beliefs change too. We need to be open to change, open to trying new ways, better ways of doing things. If we are not open to change, we remain stuck in our old ways; all the while, the world has moved on and we have chosen to remain behind. We must keep up to date with what is happening around us in the world, always looking for better ways to improve our lives. Lastly, I know it's cliché; however, I have found that lessons will keep repeating themselves in all areas of life until the lesson is truly learned and our reactions and behaviours are changed for the better. Lessons that are learned and followed up with changed behaviours direct us on the right path for transformation to become the best version of ourselves. It's very important to understand that this isn't a one-off lesson; new lessons will continue to come throughout your life; it's a never-ending process of becoming until your last breath.

Value Yourself

To experience the highest form of self-value and appreciation of your own self-worth, you must first begin with understanding who you are and who you are not. By this, I mean discover your strengths and equally your weaknesses, which are just as important. You need to understand where you do well and where you don't do so well. What are you willing to learn in order to be a better version of yourself? In addition, you need to know your character. What type of person are you? What are your good points? What are you not so good points? What would you like to change to be a better version of yourself? Another important self-assessment is to know what's stopping you and holding you back, and how will you address those things, as well as knowing what's worth keeping and what needs to be released.

Once you understand your strengths and weaknesses in skill and character, you then need to make a decision and take action to improve what you're willing to change in order to become the best version of yourself. If there is anything else that you are not able to achieve on your own, find your team to make up for what you cannot be and don't want to be. This team you build up will support you in becoming the best version of yourself. Your team should consist of who you choose to have in your life. There's a quote that I love by Hans F. Hansen: **"People inspire you or they drain you – pick them wisely".** We all have different people or different things that meet different needs. It's not selfish to take care of yourself, it's OK to keep people or things that support and inspire you and eliminate or minimise contact with toxic, energy-draining people or things.

I like to think that people or things in our lives are simply in the 'good bucket' or in the 'bad bucket'. If you can't decide which bucket someone or something sits in, ask yourself if you feel good when you walk away. If you feel good, it's a keeper – if it doesn't, toss it. Now, from experience, I'm the first to admit this is easier said than done, and I'm sure that many of you would agree. What I have learned through experience is that when I have self-value, I no longer tolerate behaviour that is not aligned with my purpose and direction. When I tolerate, I'm in a state of being "stuck". To get out of this state I first try to change it; if I can't change it, then I try to accept it. When I say "accept it", please know that sometimes this means a small sacrifice, and that's ok, as long as you are not sacrificing the ability to be your authentic self. If you cannot accept it, then comes the hardest thing you need to do, and that is to let it go. Until you let it go, you cannot move forward. It's like taking one step forward and three steps back, dancing around on the spot. You cannot change what you cannot control, and if you cannot change it and you cannot accept it, then the only thing left that can give you peace is to let it go and move forward without being held back.

I cannot stress enough how this is the biggest and most critical step that will change your life. Letting things and people go does not mean that life will be one big positive journey - you will always have challenges to face - however, you are better each time, as you are wiser and choose your battles from a state of self-worth. When you know your worth, you're on a high energy frequency. You know 'if it doesn't flow, let it go'. This doesn't mean it will be easy. You will lose people and things that once occupied a very special place in your life. It will hurt and you may never be the same again, but more importantly, you will learn the lesson. If you're lucky, you will have closure. If you're not so lucky, it's not the end of the world...you do what you need to do to bring closure within yourself.

Decide And Take Action

Once you have learned your life lessons and you live from a place of knowing your self-worth, in order to achieve your desired results, you will need to take action. However, as we all know from experience, knowing when to take action and following through can be easier said than done. We may know what we want...or do we really? Go back and remember all the things that you wanted to do at one stage in your life yet never ended up doing. Now think of the things that you wanted to do and actually did them. I have looked back many times to figure out why I took action on some goals and not on others, even though I had every intention to start and had every desire to achieve.

It's not enough to just want something and to know what you need to do to reach your target. First, you need to make a decision. This decision is not a "maybe", "one day" or "someday" decision. This decision I'm talking about is a "I must", "I will" and "I am" type of decision. Knowing you have made a solid decision is still not enough though to drive you to action. The last deciding factor, the missing piece of the puzzle that I have found determines whether or not you will take the first step and continue until your goal is achieved, came to me through a quote and suddenly, it all made sense. Thank you Mr. W. Clement Stone for sharing that **"Definiteness of purpose is the starting point of all achievement"**. You need to know your so-called "Why", and you need to know how your "Why" aligns with your purpose in life to make sure that you are on the right path to live an authentic, fulfilled life that's unique to your individual needs. Knowing your purpose without any doubt in your mind will help you make a decision. This decision, with the foundation of all your lessons learned from your old story and your new self-value and respect, is what will ultimately drive you to take action and achieve success with confidence, certainty and faith, as you are on the right track and aligned to your definite purpose to help you arrive in your new story.

We are human, after all. We all fluctuate in our levels of motivation, our confidence and our emotional states. We all make mistakes. Sometimes we learn, sometimes we don't. We are not perfect, there is always room for improvement. Life is full of ups and downs, redirections and obstacles. Think about it, who do you know that has not had some sort of suffering or loss among the winnings in life? In every household, every individual has felt some form of loss, and every time that we have suffered, with all the bravery we can muster, we have had to deal with the situation and have needed to get back up again and again after each fall, as many times as needed. These losses, as harsh as they may have been, have taught us valuable lessons. These so-called losses have taught us to value ourselves, and they've ultimately moulded us into who we are becoming, as we will always be a "work in progress". We need to constantly revise and refine what we have been doing by continuously finding ways to do it better and to be better.

When you have a definite purpose in life and have made a concrete decision that there are no excuse buckets, it's like standing on an empty field - there is no limit on what you can do and no limit on the distance that you can go. When you take action towards your purpose which is what your born to do, it doesn't feel like work, it's not a quick band-aid fix. It's not a job, it is your life; and when you are really living, time speeds up and your energy levels soar. When you're in this state, how you are in one area of life will flow to every area of life. At any moment, we can make a decision and take action; however, true transformation ignites when this decision is made on a foundation of purpose, learnings and self-value. When we are on the right track and taking actions, it's amazing how life delivers who we need and what we need, almost so perfectly timed, as if a higher existence is conspiring towards our guaranteed success. And once we've reached success, we look back and reflect, and suddenly we can see how the puzzle was put together with perfectly timed events and destined interactions. With each success we become a little wiser and emerge with restored faith in a truly magical existence which helps us to remember that we hold the key to our lives in becoming the best, authentic version of ourselves. We've always held that key, and we always will.

"And suddenly you just know it's time to start something new and trust the magic of beginning."

~ Meister Eckhart

CHAPTER TEN

Passion Drives A New Beginning

By Sandy Escabi

The necessity of adapting yourself to a new system where suddenly you have to rebuild and change your life again! That is my transformation.

This happens to all of us under different circumstances, like starting a new business, going to college, living in a new place, starting a new job, undergoing a change of status, family loss, etc. Life challenges you so many times and in different circumstances. Sometimes, you are in a place where you don't speak the language, you don't have your usual work status, you missed your books, friends, family, and you don't even know how to drive a car. Well, it happened to me, but it was the change that made my life better.

I have to confess, it has been challenging to write this chapter because I have to go back and think of who I was all those years ago, all I had back then, what I brought with me, what I gained over the years, who I lost, and who I've become.

I was a twenty-four-year old girl who was full of energy, a girl who had always tried to be a good daughter.

At that time, I was teaching 56 third-graders at a school during the morning, and I was also a professor at a university, where I was teaching education, helping my students to write their theses and supervising their internships. As a hobby, I had my professional dance group, and we were doing presentations at the university where I worked, and I was studying towards my master's degree in History Education. As you can see, I was dedicated to my profession and to helping my students the best way I could.

One day I called my mom, who was in the United States, and I told her that I wanted to become a nun in the Catholic school where I was working at the time. "A nun?!" she said. That same week she bought me a ticket to Florida in an attempt to convince me not to become a nun. I couldn't refuse an opportunity to see my family, so I boarded a plane to the United States.

Visiting my family was a shocking and awakening experience. It was a month full of memories and emotion.

It was unbelievable for me to witness how the economic situation in Colombia had affected my family.

My parents had seven clothing boutiques and a factory in Colombia, and for most of the time, life was good. Unfortunately, once Colombia started to import inexpensive clothing and other goods from China, domestic industry began to suffer. Local businesses could not compete with the low prices of the newly imported Chinese items, and they went out of business. Our family was among those who were affected. Before we knew it, our stores failed and we had to sell everything. That was when my father decided to move the family to the United States. My half-sisters sent him American residency papers so that he could easily start a new life in the United States.

I stayed behind and sold our house, the stores, furniture, everything. All of the personal items were placed in storage to be collected at a later time. I thought I was doing the difficult part by selling all the memories of my life away, but I was wrong.

When I went up to the United States to visit my parents, I was shocked. They were working janitorial and housekeeping jobs. I couldn't understand why my father wasn't a realtor, an accountant, or a manager, jobs he could have easily received back in Colombia.

The new lifestyle had taken its toll on my father. He went from being strong and energetic to thin and tired. He had lost so much weight because of the high-paced, uncomfortable, rough style of life here in the United States.

The trip wasn't all bad, though! During my vacation, my parents introduced me to their friends. One of their friends, Peter, gave me a tour around Florida. We tried food from different countries. We danced and laughed! Honestly, it was a magical experience. Sometimes I felt like I was in a dream.

Unfortunately, the day arrived when I left the family again. I had to go back to Colombia, back home again where my real life was waiting. Vacation was over.

I arrived in the capital, Bogotá. While I'd had so much fun in the States, I had seen how hard my parents worked. Their hard work created an appreciation for each opportunity that life was giving me and made me love my profession more. I realized that, in order to obtain what you desire, you have to work for it. I decided to continue with my plan of teaching. I wrote books and became the Dean of the History Department after my training.

Time passed, and one day while I was in Colombia, I suddenly received a phone call from this charming guy, Peter, who said, "Hey, I'm at the airport. I want you to show me the book you wrote, take me to the university where you work, and all of that. Show me everything you said you have been doing here. Is it really true?" Personally, this sounded kind of weird to me, but I thought, *Why not? He was great company in Orlando, so let's welcome this guy home!* So, my aunt and my extended family welcomed my friend, and after a little tour of the city, we travelled to Villa de Leyva, which was a safe town at that time.

While we were in that beautiful villa, he asked me to date him. I said yes, and we started traveling more often. Then, in our travels, he asked me to live with my parents in Orlando so that we could get to know each other better. It was a difficult decision, but I wanted to try. Plus, that way I could spend more time with my parents, as well as learn more English. So, I agreed, and I left behind my three jobs and my family and friends for an adventure, and for love.

I left feeling like I was just going for another vacation. I left all doors open and waiting for my return.

After several months of dating, Peter asked me to move in with him. I said yes! We fell in love. This was a scandal for my family, but it felt right at the time. So, time passed, and later Peter took me to the beach and asked me to marry him.

We agreed that we wanted something non-religious, and so we had a small wedding. My dress was gorgeous. The garden was perfect. We had violins, some boleros (a romantic type of music), and my father walked me down the aisle. My sister arrived for the wedding, and we went to a fancy restaurant.

Well, while all of that sounds great, what I hadn't realized was that, in real life, moving to another country wasn't easy. It wasn't as simple as saying "and they lived happily ever after…" This is how I ended up here in Florida getting homesickness, missing my jobs, friends, and much more.

Life Isn't Like Disney Movies

What really happens when you move to a different country is that you realize how many adjustments you need to make in order to succeed. I needed to believe in myself, to challenge circumstances, to look for success again, and not to look back.

It's not easy, but one step at a time, you can conquer every obstacle in your path. This is the time to ask yourself what you want, even though it isn't in front of you at that moment.

It may sound strange, but coming from South America, people always talk about the land of opportunities, "The American Dream." The reality is that being a foreigner is extremely hard and you never fit in, but nothing can stop your desire to be part of the new system once you settle in.

Adjusting to my current situation and believing in my instincts to survive, to go beyond my situation, this became my new goal. Communication was my priority: to learn a new language and to be able to understand. So, I enrolled in English classes. I watched TV with English captions and a dictionary in my hand. I listened to English music, and I tried to order at the restaurant or speak at the supermarket with no help.

The process of learning English at school was interesting since my classmates were also from different countries, like Russia, India, etc. So, we used pictures to communicate and spoke the few English words we knew. It was then that I regretted studying French instead of English when I was in high school.

I acknowledge that the United States has amazing people, but I was used to Colombian culture, a culture that is affectionate, filled with hugs and kisses. Sayings like *"mi casa es tu casa"* (my home is your home) was not just an expression; we really meant it back home. It was a big deal to adapt to the system in the United States. I vividly remember the first time I had to give personal space, a concept that we didn't have back home.

Apparently, I was too affectionate for the American system.

In Florida I had to learn new rules and customs. I was missing the museums and the fast pace of the city. Suddenly, I found myself in a town with very hot weather, learning to distinguish one snake from another, and surrounded by nature, beaches, and theme parks.

To be able to survive in this system, you can't take one step back...only steps forward.

You should not overanalyze the concept of freedom when you are adjusting, because little aspects of normal freedom from your past perspective will become a luxury. I had to learn how to drive a car, something that I didn't need to do back in my country. In Colombia, I could walk to go to the supermarket or to go to work. While here in Florida, you must have a car for everything. Having a car is part of your basic needs, like having a job.

I would never have thought that, to be able to live and work somewhere different than your place of origin, you would need to be called "legal." So, I started getting my working papers and going through immigration requirements. First temporary residency, then residency, then transferring, plus translating all my degrees, and more. I had to start from zero. But, little by little, my family and Peter helped me to make the process as smooth as possible. Sometimes Peter's sister gave me company and transportation. And calling my friends in Colombia helped me to go through all of this. I was getting ready for the U.S.

Some people would say I was lucky, but nobody really knew how many times I wanted to take an airplane and go back. I noticed that I had love, but I had lost my identity. Following my now-ex-husband's directions all the time wasn't easy. After one year, the boat was shaken, and it was time to wipe my tears and get even stronger.

This process took a while. But to be honest, after 20 years of living in the United States, I understand that this country isn't perfect. But nothing is perfect, and I love this country: the safety, nature, people, and opportunities.

This is the place where, 19 years ago, I became a mother. My son has made me the happiest and most blessed person in the world. It was a blessing to see that my son was healthy after I'd gone through a difficult pregnancy. I was ready to do whatever it took to move forward and create a wonderful home for him. My son lit up my life and gave me a purpose, a reason to continue, and a reason to be in the United States.

When you have a child, you concentrate all your energy on what is next. First it was walking, then teething, first words, Boy Scouts, soccer games, bowling tournaments, family celebrations, and more. Every day is a surprise. However, after a while I realized that what I really wanted was to be an excellent example for my son and to grow professionally again. I began to try to rediscover myself by looking for a job, hopefully in my profession—helping others and teaching—again.

For a lot of people that sounds ridiculous. "Find a job in your profession?" they would say. "You could get a job cleaning! You're an immigrant!" Well, I was a professor at the University of Colombia. I knew I could work to have that profession here. So, one day after another year of learning and being a mom and a wife, I realized that I wanted to teach again!

I bought the newspaper and, while translating with a dictionary, I found an ad for a Spanish teacher. I went with my bad English and knocked at the door to see what would happen. Plus, I was getting tired of listening to "When are you going to get a job?" from my now-ex-husband.

It felt like I was jumping into a strange world. My aunt was visiting for vacation during this time, and she stayed with my son while I embarked on this exciting adventure. They decided to interview me, and I got the job!

I called Mom and my sister, and they agreed to help me. They would take turns in their free time to take care of the baby while I worked. When Peter arrived home that day, he started complaining because I didn't have a job. He thought I was just joking when I told him the great news. He couldn't believe that I had just gotten a job teaching 500 students, kindergarten through eighth grade, and he replied, "But the baby?" I explained that everything was going to be okay, and I had it under control.

After I started working at the school, I sent all my academic transcripts to Tallahassee to obtain my Spanish teaching certificate. The school fell in love with my lesson plans and asked me to create the Spanish program for the school. Eventually, my son became a student in that private school for free.

It was a great experience. Students taught me a lot of English while I taught them Spanish culture, songs, and art. Later on, I even helped with the marketing of the school.

I'm grateful that this school believed in my ability and gave me the opportunity to succeed. The administration cooperated in helping me to become accredited and allowed me to develop their Spanish program. This is how I started teaching again. Over the years, I taught Spanish at colleges, private Schools, and ESOL programs.

Another important aspect in transitions is to free your mind and open your heart to a world full of positive possibilities. Working out and breathing deeply, being sweet, continuing to offer your warm smile, and being a loving person after so many years of dealing with culture shock...these are the keys to this process.

Personally, having a family, teaching my students, and volunteering in the community has helped me to understand that I'm still learning. I'm grateful for this process and the daily life lessons that come with it.

It was the ability to rediscover my values and inspirations while I was watching my son succeed that let me transform. He always brings me peace, motivation, kindness, and especially inspiration. As you can see, not everything was lost. I brought with me faith in God, strength to accomplish anything, and self-confidence. So, please don't forget who you are, your passions and skills. It helps you to define who you are going to be. And destroy the stereotype that, if you go to a foreign country, you have to work in construction, cleaning, or things like that...I proved that belief wrong!

Sometimes, even if you try to start a new life, your passion, your essence, your interests, education, and soul will never change. My dad always said, *"tu titulo no te lo quita nadie."* "Nobody can take your degree away from you," and he was right.

I remember that my beautiful sister helped me to make my vision board. It was awesome and helpful. It reaffirmed my professional and personal values as a human being.

Peter suggested that I read the book *Seven Habits of Highly Effective People* by Stephen Covey, and I found it to be very proactive. It showed me another way to look at my life and focus on myself again.

Starting new projects to continue forward is part of the equation. Don't be stuck. Stimulate your mind with knowledge and the desire to continue evolving. I studied for my master's degree and became a citizen of the United States while I was working. It took a lot of discipline.

Please understand that you are perfectly imperfect, and you deserve to be loved. To be honest, I have to remember this, and I still have to work on a few things here and there, especially after my father passed away due to cancer and my relationship with Peter was gone. But that is a story for another day. As you can see, other situations affected my journey. However, all my family's support over the years and the desire to be an educator are still important.

Your passion and inspirations are those little hidden things that will help you to start a new life, making your transformation a success. Those values all together become your soul, your strength, and the beginning of your journey to continue with your life.

Have family, coworkers, good relationships with your mom, sister, or friends. Have faith in God, the universe, or the future; have some kind of spiritual connection. These are necessary. I personally think that getting involved with the community and volunteering for different organizations was a huge help for this adaptation during my transition.

Suddenly, I realized who I had become. I'm a mother and a citizen of this new country where I get to help people from all over the world through different organizations. I'm a teacher who has been writing Spanish programs for colleges and private schools for 18 years. I really don't know what is coming after this, maybe a new career, hobbies, or hopefully a romantic relationship. But I do know that there is a lot to discover and a lot to learn.

So, you certainly are able to start a new adventure and transform your life again if you are willing to do it.

From the bottom of my heart, I really hope this chapter helps some immigrants like me to transform their lives while they continue with their passions and find the strength to be themselves again.

Let's cooperate to obtain success and open our minds and hearts towards transformation. Be part of the new system, because adaptation is possible, and you will realize that what you've always wanted to do is there wherever you go.

Rediscover your passions! Don't let them vanish! Transformation is an awesome and positive experience that is always possible!

Believe in yourself.

You came to this world with a mission. Persistence is a virtue. Let's use that virtue!

"Transformations can feel exhausting - but that's because your draining out old energies which no longer serve you, to make room for the new."

~ Vex King

CHAPTER ELEVEN

From Sick And Tired to Healthy And Wealthy

By Nikki Galagher

Ever since I was a little girl I always wondered what I would be like when I grew up. Now that I'm grown up, I wonder what the rest of my life will be like. You see, we never know what tomorrow can bring; what adventure, what surprise, what mystery will unfold tomorrow. No one knows, and that is what makes life so amazing.

> **"Yesterday is history; tomorrow a mystery. Today is a gift – that is why it is called the Present."**
>
> ~Alice Morse Earle.

As a child, it seemed like Christmas was never going to arrive, and the time between school holidays felt like an eternity. As an adult, I seem to be packing down the

Christmas tree when it is time to set up again. Is it just me, or is time absolutely flying by the older we get?

In the 40 years I have been on this planet, I have had many truly amazing days. I have also had many days when I just did not want to get out of bed in the morning. We all have those days. If only it could be Sunday morning every day, when the alarm clock didn't go off, when I don't have to fight traffic, when I don't need to be around other people and I can just stay in my own little world in bed with nothing but beautiful dreams to entertain me all day long.

For the last ten years, I have wanted to have more Doona days (staying in bed with just the Doona) than I have ever had before; that is because ten years ago I was diagnosed with a rare brain disease called Intracranial Hypertension, or IH, for short. This is a condition that has no cause and no cure yet!

My brain makes too much spinal fluid that puts pressure on my brain, and causes daily headaches that often turn into migraines. Having a headache 24/7 is, at times, unbearable. Imagine waking up with the worst hangover you've ever had, knowing that you are going to feel like this all day, all week, all month, all year, and for many years to come, until they find a cure.

Before I had surgery and had a VP shunt inserted in my brain to drain off the excess fluid, the only relief I got from the feeling that my head was being squashed in a vice was having regular lumbar punctures, which means a 15cm needle is inserted into my spine to drain out the excess spinal fluid. The only problem with this is that it is extremely painful, and if they take out too much fluid, I suffer from a low-pressure headache, which is just as bad, if not worse, than having a high-pressure headache. A low-pressure headache feels like your brain has been sucked dry of all the fluids and it feels like it is caving in; versus a high-pressure headache, which feels like it's going to explode.

At last count, I'm up to six brain surgeries, 31 lumbar punctures, eight MRI's, hundreds of CT scans, and so many X-Rays I should glow in the dark by now. I'm not telling this to get sympathy and to make you to think "Poor Nikki! That's so terrible". I'm sharing this with you so that I can share with you my strength, my courage, my passion and my gratitude.

I could sit in the corner and cry, "Poor me! Why did this have to happen to me? Life just isn't fair", but that wouldn't get me anywhere. The crying and the stress only make my headaches worse.

I tell you this so that you will get off your ass and stop your whining about the little things in your life that seem so insignificant when you see the things that I have seen. I am here to motivate and inspire you to live your most amazing life possible. I am here to be your wake-up call to be grateful for everything in your life; to be grateful for everything you DO have in your life, as well as to be grateful for all the things that you DO NOT have in your life.

Having brain surgery is a really scary thing to go through, and even at the time, I put on a super brave face and pretended I was ok with it. But deep down, I was shitting myself; I didn't want to die. I had too much to live for. What if the doctor sneezes while he has a scalpel inside of my brain and cuts something that he is not supposed to? What if I don't wake up? What if they decide that cos the shunts keep braking inside my head that I shouldn't have one and I have to go back to having Lumber Punctures every four weeks? All these crazy thoughts went through my head before every surgery. When I woke up from each surgery in recovery, I would move my hands and feet and make sure everything still worked. A tear of gratitude would roll down my cheek as I thanked the universe and my angels for protecting me during the surgery.

Growing up, my parents had always taught me to say please and thank you and I always thought of myself as a grateful person, but it was not until I was 31 years old and in hospital after my first brain surgery that I really understood the power of it. I was in a four-bed room in Liverpool Hospital in Sydney's western suburbs where I met Angela, who was recovering from a brain aneurysm. She was sitting up in bed a few days after major surgery to save her life. Angela also had a beautiful half head of shaved hair and 40 plus staples. She was missing hair from ear to ear across the top, while mine was back right side of my head. (Between the two of us, we had a whole head of hair!)

The gentleman next to Angela (who was diagonally opposite me) had also had a brain aneurysm, but he had been about 40 minutes away from the hospital, and by the time he got on the operating table, unfortunately, it was too late. The aneurysm had burst, and he was now going to spend the rest of his life hooked up to feeding tubed, breathing tubes, and a colostomy bag.

Angela was very lucky and grateful that she got to the hospital in time, as a few minutes later, her life could have been very different.

I remember that moment everyday when I wake up cos no matter how much pain I am in or what problems or challenges I'm facing, I'm always so grateful that I woke up, that I can feed myself, that I can walk, that I can talk, that I can breathe on my own, and most of all that I can wipe my own ass. Those simple things, we can all take for granted. Well, I don't take them for granted anymore. I know that life could've dealt me a totally different hand and as crappy as my condition gets at times and as much pain as I have, I'm so very grateful that I still have so much to be grateful for.

Throughout my life, I have had many reasons to be very depressed and even suicidal; being overweight all through high school and getting picked on daily, being diagnosed with a rare brain disease at the age of 30 and being told I could be blind by the age of 40, having six brain surgeries, almost going bankrupt, loosing $30K in a bad business deal, being dumped by more guys than any other woman I know, living in chronic pain everyday... the list goes on. But even after all the heartache in my life, I still wake up daily with a smile on my face because I am alive, and I thank the universe everyday for these basic gifts that millions of people around the world are not so lucky to be able to experience. If I focus on all the pain and heartache I have had over the years, I would have a massive pity party and be loaded up with drugs just to cope, but that is not what I choose to focus on each day.

I have spent the last 15 years attending personal development seminars all over the world and even worked in the industry for about four years, so I've listened to thousands of hours of speakers sharing their journeys and life lessons of how they have overcome challenges and obstacles that life had thrown their way. Almost all of them mention gratitude as playing an important part in their success.

For the last ten years, I have been volunteering for a charity called Magic Moments Basket Brigade. We pack and deliver Christmas hampers for families who are struggling financially. It is a charity that I'm very passionate about, as I know what its like to struggle to make ends meet.

I don't have any kids myself and I can't imagine what it would be like to be struggling at Christmas and not have enough money to put food on the table, let alone putting toys under the tree. Our amazing volunteers collect donations of food and toys and deliver them anonymously to families nominated by organisations who have been working with the families and know that they are doing it tough. Our hampers are designed to let them know that they are cared for and not forgotten about at Christmas, and to give them a hand up not a hand out.

When you spend time helping others that are less fortunate than yourself, your own problems don't seem as big, and knowing that other people are relying on you helps you push through and go that extra mile. The problem was, I didn't know how to say no. I was always helping everyone else and left no time to look after myself, so 2017 was a year of self-destruction for me and I burnt myself out. I was the National Coordinator for Basket Brigade helping ten brigades, which helped over 5,000 families at Christmas. I was also coordinating my own local brigade, where with a committee of just two of us, we fed over 150 families.

I had put on 15kg since the Christmas before, and my relationship had gone downhill, and we broke up just after Christmas 2017. I was broke, broken (physically and mentally), and emotionally exhausted. Neither of us had the money to move out, so we had to do what many separated couples do and live together in separate rooms while trying to heal. Those first few weeks were really tough and I don't now how I actually got through it. But I did. "I've done it before and I can do it again", I kept telling myself.

During that time, Mark was diagnosed with Lymes Disease, which explained a lot of his behaviour over the last 12 months and why he was so disconnected due to the brain fog. "It wasn't my fault", or "His bloody Lyme Disease"...at least I had something to blame. Mark suggested that I go and see his naturopath to check if I also had it, as I had many of the same symptoms (but they are also the same as my IH symptoms) - brain fog, headaches, forgetfulness, etc. Better to be safe than sorry.

I turned 40 on Jan 31st and it was a huge turning point in my life. I was not where I had expected to be when I was 40: single, broke, driving a car that was falling apart, still renting, in debt, and overweight.

I booked in to see Isabel the naturopath, and even though it was a two-hour drive, she was so worth it. I attended her clinic on Valentines day - Self Love day - and that is the day that would change my life forever.

Isabel uses a biofeedback machine, which scans the body using 9,000 frequencies to detect weaknesses such as viruses, nutritional deficiencies, allergies, toxins, abnormalities and food sensitivities. During the two-hour session, it picked up a whole range of things wrong with my body including Adrenal Fatigue, because I had been running myself into the ground looking after everyone else for the last 12 months and not looking after myself. I also have Epstein Barr Virus; I had never even heard of it. Apparently lots of people have it, but it can lay dormant in your body until a major life event like a death in the family, break up, or loss of job triggers it, and then you develop a stage-four condition, which a doctor may diagnose with Lupus, Fibromylaga, Chronic Fatigue, MS, Arthritis, and so many more. I highly suggest that you read the book *Medical Medium* by Anthony William if you have any type of chronic condition. That book is a game-changer. I knew from that moment on that I was going to have to make some massive changes in my life if I didn't want to end up with one of the above chronic conditions.

Just before my 40th birthday, I got a case of food poisoning and had the runs from 9am until midnight, when I had to call the home doctor out. It was horrible, and over the next few weeks I felt so rough. I decided to stay away from chicken and other meats for awhile, just while my body healed. I decided to become vegetarian for the next two weeks. My body really liked this new way of eating, as everything that was going in was really healthy and I needed to nourish my body from the roller coaster it had been on.

My best friend was vegan, and as I hardly ate any dairy anyway, it was easy for me to become vegan too. My only problem was that I still loved chocolate and vegan chocolate is really expensive. So as usual, I decided to do things my way - I call myself a 95% vegan. I had been on hundreds of diets my whole life and every one of them always made me feel like I was depriving myself of the food I loved, and I knew if I was going to turn my life around, I had to make some massive changes in deciding what foods I actually did love and what ones were good for my body. I had spent 40 years trashing my body and now it was time to treat it like the temple that it is.

I used to suffer from reflux whenever I ate bread or pasta so I removed them from my diet. I now only eat quinoa or pulse pasta, made from beans, chick peas, and lentils. I removed all dairy products, except for the occasional bit of chocolate, so that I don't feel like I'm on a diet. There are great non-dairy alternatives for things like butter and ice-cream like Nuttilex and sorbet. I even make my own from coconut milk by removing all processed sugar (anything in a packet). I still eat lots of fruit, as fruit is very healing for your body. I eliminated all meat and processed meats, and for the first few months, I only had a small 100g serve of organic lamb or salmon about every ten days. I really love these two and felt that by keeping them in I was not depriving myself as I use them as a treat. I didn't feel the need to eat meat every day as I feel it clogs my body up. For two months now, I have been full vegan and my body is loving it.

I juice fresh fruit and veggies every morning and have at least three litres of Alkalised Kangan water everyday, and this routine has helped me release 12kg in the last four months with only one workout a week. Having Adrenal Fatigue, I have to be careful not to overdo it at the gym, as I don't want to burn myself out, so I just have one personal training session a week to help me tone and tighten and strengthen my body.

I am 1/3 of my way towards my goal to where I want to be, but this time I know I will achieve it unlike all the other times I have tried in the past to release weight - mainly due to the fact that I don't see myself on a diet and this is now a way of life. This is how I choose to live the rest of my life, and I no longer wish to fill my body with all the toxic junk food that I once did. I'm just taking it easy and not trying to get any quick fixes. I know that, as I have spent 40 years putting crap into my body, it's not realistic to think that it will all release in a few months. It's going to take time, and I'm cool with that. My daily focus is just to keep moving forward and not let the next 40 years be like the last 40.

I'm not trying to get skinny or to look great like the photoshopped magazine pictures or catwalk models; I'm just wanting to be healthier and fitter. I'm sick of getting out of breath when walking up flights of stairs and not being able to do certain things. The most embarrassing moments for me over the years were every time I used to fly (which was a lot), I would have to ask for the seat belt extender cos the normal seatbelt would not do up around my belly. I would usually discreetly ask the cabin crew as I was boarding to bring one down to me once seated, and many times I've seen the look of pity or disgust on the other passengers' faces when the crew handed me the special "fat belt". At my largest, I was a size 22-24 and it is not easy being that big in society; and not only do we give ourselves a hard time, but so do others without even realising they are doing it.

I feel very blessed that for the last seven years I have worked for City Chic - a Plus-sized clothing store that creates beautiful clothes for women of all shapes between sizes 14-24; and over the years, I have had thousands of conversations with women who come into my store to buy clothes, not knowing how to style their body for their shape. I love it when my ladies walk out feeling fabulous, sexy, and beautiful and looking amazing.

I have spent so many wasted hours feeling badly about myself, talking negatively about myself, and having a bad body image, while trying to put on the happy face.

I have come full circle on my weight gain-weight loss-weight gain-weight loss journey, and I'm finally in a good place now at 40.

It bloody took me long enough, where I can look in the mirror at my size 16-18 body that is covered in scars, cellulite, stretch marks, uneven skin, pimples and wrinkles and much more, and I can look in the mirror standing there as naked as the day I was born and tell myself:

"I LOVE YOU - YOU ARE BEAUTIFUL."

I know that the value on the scales does not matter; it does NOT represent my value as a human. It does not show your worth as a person. You are so much more than your body.

Repeat after me...

"I am NOT FAT - I have fat."

Let me repeat that, "I AM NOT FAT I HAVE FAT."

Just like I have fingernails, I AM NOT fingernails.

"I am not defined by something that I carry on my body, like hair or fingernails."

You are so much more than the weight you carry on your body.

I define myself by my character:

- my values
- my beliefs

- my contribution to my community
- my love for my family and friends
- my volunteer work
- my morals
- my attributes
- my character
- my personality
- my quick wit
- my street smarts
- my social skills
- my sense of humour
- my pride
- my sense of style
- my sensuality
- my charisma
- my flirty nature
- my adventurous spirit
- my gratitude for life
- my strength of character
- my motivation
- and so many more wonderful attributes

The kilos on the scales are just a small part of what makes me who I am, and if people are going to judge me, make comments or criticise me because of my weight or my body shape, then I say, "Buddy there is the door, and don't let it hit you on the ass on your way out!"

If you struggle with the same issues, please stop putting yourself down and know you are really amazing. So let me drill it into your head again:

You are enough, you are beautiful inside and out, and you are worthy of a zillion times more greatness that you can ever dream possible. It's your life, your body, and you only have one shot at living your most abundant life possible. Grab it with both hands, hold on, and enjoy the ride.

Over the years, I have seen friends struggle with infertility, while others complained about the stretch marks they received from being pregnant. It was a massive a-ha moment when I realised that my friends who were not able to have kids would LOVE to have a body covered in stretch marks if it meant they were blessed with a child they so desperately wanted. It's all about perspective. So the next time you look at your body and your first thought is to be ashamed of your stretch marks, reverse your thinking, as they are stripes of honour, showing that you were blessed to grow a precious little baby in your belly. So be proud of your stretch marks as they created life!

I am grateful to wake up everyday, and I feel so blessed to be alive that I'm not going to waste time and energy that I don't have, stressing over how big my bum looks in this dress, because I'm going to shake my bootie no matter what size it is. I have no issues getting on the dance floor and getting my groove on.

They say confidence is the sexiest thing a woman can wear. I would have to agree, as the feeling of empowerment I now have cannot be described in words. I learned how to strip back all those layers of conditioning and society stereotyping crap that is layered upon us from a very early age - we can be liberated.

We can be released from the pressures of how we should think, what we should wear, how we should act, what we should buy, who we should be, and how we should behave. It's time to love ourselves in all our glory. How can we expect anyone else to love, respect, and worship our bodies if we don't love ourselves first?

So it's time to treat our bodies like a temple, cut out the crap, tell ourselves everyday "You are worthy and amazing", have sex with the lights on (Go on, I dare you!), be adventurous, do something you haven't done before, do something you used to love to do as a kid...because life is too short to work all the time and have no fun. We need to enjoy life; it's meant to be lived.

You don't want to get to 60, 70 or 80 and have a long list of things you should have done when you were younger. Do them now while you have the chance.

What if your doctor told you that you only had 30 days left to live? Would you spend the next 30 days doing the same things you did in the last 30 days? I'm guessing not.

Would you travel more?

Visit family and friends?

Make up with that person you have a disagreement with?

Would you tick off items on your bucket list?

Would you write that book you have been putting off?

Would you tell people what they really mean to you?

Why do you need to wait until you have a death sentence to LIVE your life? Why not do it starting today?

Have you seen the movie *The Holiday* with Queen Latifah? It's awesome. She lived a very normal life eating cardboard microwave meals, too afraid to ask the hot guy out and never going anywhere - until she finds out that she is dying - then she lives her best life possible and takes more risks than she has ever taken in her life. It's a wonderful movie.

So what are your next 30 days going to look like?

Take out a note pad and create a bucket list of things to achieve, do or experience over the next 30 days, 90 days, 6 months and 12 months.

I have always had many hopes and dreams and things I've wanted to tick off my bucket list, but ever since I can remember, I have always struggled financially; that is, until recently. Earlier this year, I saw a post on a friend's Facebook page talking about how he had just joined a 90% automated platform where most of the work was already done. He wrote about how I would not have to do any sales calls, didn't have to harass my friends or family, didn't have to do in-home parties or presentations (like I had done for three and a half years with another company). And even though it sounded to good to be true, I put my skepticism aside and jumped on board for the risk-free trial and I have not looked back. I am making crazy amounts of money, and I'm not even doing any sales calls or doing any selling. We have coaches that take care of that for me. Yesterday I made more money while having an afternoon nanna nap than most people do working a 40-hour work week. It's all online and mostly automated. I still have to do some work, but it's fun and I love it. I've spent my whole life trying to find my passion, and who would have thought I would find it on Facebook in my PJ's?

Living in Melbourne, it gets very cold for at least half the year, so PJ's are regular wardrobe for me. I love that I can stay at home and make money in my PJ's. With my brain condition too, I never know when my next surgery is going to be, so having a business that is flexible enough to cater for me to work from the comfort of my home or from a hospital bed, means that I don't have to worry about having to take time off my casual job. I can go back to work after surgery or a hospital visit when I'm ready to and not when I have to, just cos I have to pay the bills. It breaks my heart that there are so many sick people out there who are forced to work just to pay the bills. My goal is to help as many people as I can to achieve a "PJ's Lifestyle" or "Bikini Lifestyle", depending on where in the world you live!

This year has been a massive transformation for me, and I feel like a butterfly that has spent many years trapped in a cocoon and now I have grown my wings and its time for me to fly.

I truly believe that everyone has the capacity to spread their wings and fly too.

- It just takes consistent effort.
- Being the best version of yourself everyday.
- Living with gratitude everyday.
- Daily rituals of learning.
- Self love & self care.
- Taking risks.
- Modeling from people who have been successful and achieved the things you want to achieve.
- Believing in yourself.
- Having courage.

- Claiming your greatness.
- Creating more of everything you want in you life.
- Reading for a minimum of 30 minutes everyday, about your area of expertise/passion.
- Listening to audio books daily.
- Putting great nutrition into your body.
- And treating your body like the temple that it is.

What I have learned over the last 40 years is...

- The universe never gives you anything you are not strong enough to handle and the more pain you go though, the stronger you become.
- Don't hold onto pain. Feel it and release it as it builds up in your body, as it causes dis-ease and you will get sick.
- Forgiving people who have hurt you does not mean that you forgive their behaviour; it just means that you are no longer emotionally chained to that person and you have released them from your life.
- Live with compassion & kindness.
- Treat people like you would like to be treated.
- Don't worry about what other people think of you - it only matters what you think about yourself.

- Love yourself and cherish that inner child inside of you.

- Feed great things into your body and also into your mind.

- Turn off the TV and educate yourself. There are so many amazing books to read and to listen to. Self-education is the most important education you can have, and you have started by reading this book - so "Well done! I'm proud of you."

- A day without learning is a day wasted.

So now it's time to work on your transformational change!

What are you going to change?

Live with Passion, Purpose, Love & Gratitude

"Transformation

is a journey

without a

final destination"

~ Marilyn Ferguson

Author Biographies

John Spender

Chapter One

John Spender didn't learn how to read and write at a basic level until he was 10 years old. He has since traveled the world, started many business's, leading him to create the award winning book series *A Journey Of Riches*, he is an Award Winning International Speaker and Movie Maker.

John was an international NLP trainer and has coached thousands of people from various backgrounds through all sorts of challenges. From the borderline homeless to very wealthy individuals, he has helped many people to get in touch with their truth to create a life on their terms.

John's search for answers to living a fulfilling life has take him to working with Native American Indians in the Hills of San Diego, the forests of Madagascar, swimming with humpback whales in Tonga, exploring the Okavango Delta of Botswana and the Great Wall of China. He's travelled from Chile to Slovakia, Hungary to the Solomon Islands, the mountains of Italy and the streets of Mexico.

Every where his journey has taken him, John has discovered a hunger among people to find a new way to live, with a yearning for freedom.

He also co-wrote the script for the film *Adversity* and interviewed all the guests, including Jack Canfield, Lisa Garr, Dr John DeMartini and Dr Micheal Beckwith to name a few.

For more information about contributing to the *A Journey Of Riches* series contact John via email; jrspender7@gmail.com.

John Hanna

Chapter Two

A childhood of great poverty gave him the lifelong desire to master wealth – his father died penniless at the young age of 57, never having fulfilled his great dreams.

John Hanna is the CEO and founder of numerous companies, with over 25 years experience in Finance, Financial Planning, Marketing and Property Investment. A recognised speaker in Personal Development and Wealth Creation, he has dedicated his life to the study of Financial Laws and Universal Principles in order to benefit every day hard working people, people like his mum and dad.

John has dedicated his life to the study of these Universal Principles, particularly as they relate to the creation of Financial Wealth. His desire is traveling the world sharing his knowledge and experience with everyone so that, unlike his father, people can live a life of purpose and fulfillment doing what they love, and loving what they do, being not servants to money but masters of it.

JoJo Bennington

Chapter Three

Women's Empowerment Mentor

Certified Nutrition and Wellness Coach

Network Marketing Professional

JoJo is a transformational speaker and trainer who works with six figure earners, millionaires, and aspiring entrepreneurs across the globe to move forward, promoting personal growth and overcoming obstacles. Her no-nonsense approach of honesty mixed with compassion helps people to take a candid look at themselves to discover and challenge their self imposed limits. She connects with groups through numerous retreats and weekends as a speaker and host.

For the past 13 years JoJo has honed skills in the profession of network marketing, growing a large, successful team dedicated to helping people transform their lives, bodies, and mindsets. As a Nutritional Consultant, she has studied and applied numerous modalities to help support her clients highest quality of life. She is passionate about showing people there is a better way to improve health and wealth.

JoJo co-founded Unlimited Potential Retreats (UP), and Empowering Healthy Women Calls. These events assist in healing, forgiving, finding our voice, and recognizing inner/outer beauty. These events help women move forward and stand in their power, through open dialogue, sharing experiences, and exposure to special guests.

She believes that we are the creators of our personal world, and we can have an impact by adjusting our mindset at home.

JoJo was born and raised in Las Vegas, Nevada, where she lives with her husband Vinnie.

To stay in contact with JoJo please visit her at:

jojobennington.com

https://www.facebook.com/tiptopjojo/

https://www.facebook.com/groups/empoweringhealthywomen/

Tracy Sotirakis

Chapter Four

Tracy Sotirakis is a professional makeup artist, hair stylist and educator. Her business is based out of Las Vegas, NV and Utah, but she also enjoys traveling around the country for work.

 Tracy loves the beauty business and is passionate about teaching skills to clients and other professionals. When she has time off, Tracy enjoys hiking, skiing, fishing and spending time with her loved ones.

Check out Tracy's work at www.tracysmakeup.com or her Instagram @tracysmakeup.

Tom Wind

Chapter Five

TOM WIND is an entrepreneur, author, and Christ-centered leadership consultant. As a former shaman and owner of a luxury transformational retreat center in Bali, he experienced a full rebirth in Jesus Christ and left it all behind to pursue the life of Truth and freedom.

From a young age, Tom has searched for deeper truths and more meaningful ways to live, which led him onto an intense rollercoaster of a multidimensional journey of life in Europe, the Middle East, South America, and Asia. After years of profound transformational spiritual work, he found that living in Christ is the ultimate way to heal the body, mind and soul, and to express one's full potential and purpose.

Now he travels around the world sharing his story and helping entrepreneurs and leaders to reconnect to our Lord Jesus Christ and embody their lives in the highest sense. Connect to Tom through his website www.tom-wind.com

Mia Tolis

Chapter Six
Counsellor and Educator.

Mia brings a lifetime of experience to both her educating and counselling careers. She has spent most of her time in the education industry, working as an independent consultant in the areas of personal development, leadership, management, and business, including assisting and empowering skilled professionals in finding work. Mia has post-graduate qualifications in both Education and Training, as well as Counselling.

She is passionate about human behavior and understands how and why people live the way they do. Her area of expertise is in soft skills, including topics on emotional intelligence, personal leadership, mindfulness, self-awareness, and meditation.

Mia loves learning and growing and is passionate about sharing her knowledge, wisdom, and experiences with her clients. A worldly professional, a wife, a mother to two grown-up sons, a business owner in consulting and training, and as a retail business owner of two franchises allows her to draw upon her vast life experiences.

Mia has also contributed her time and facilitated at youth camps empowering youth to believe in themselves and work towards creating a more fulfilled and compelling future.

In addition, Mia is involved with and has been trained by the world's leading peak performance coach: Tony Robbins. She has been on his leadership team for over 12 years and has travelled with him throughout Australia and the United States.

Mia's passion, dedication, and commitment are to help and support others through life's challenges. This motivates her to get up every morning, seize the day, and make a difference in other people's lives.

For more information go to www.makingchangetogether.com.au.

Stephen Smith

Chapter Seven

Stephen Smith is a man who has gone to hell and come back from the depths of darkness to a place filled with Light, Love of God and himself and others.

He made many good, but too many poor decisions that cost him everything he had. He lost businesses, two marriages, good family and friend relationships and everything else in between.

He survived a few near fatal car accidents, deadly diseases including Hepatitis C, alcohol and drug addiction.

Having for the most part lived an abundant and blessed life, he found himself fresh out of jail, homeless living in the woods and nothing but himself left. Today, he earned back most of what he lost. A real survivor, God fearing, honest, caring and compassionate person who strives to help others and give back freely in an effort to pay it forward with no expectation of reimbursement.

He strives daily to become a better person and has made a transitional change which resulted in a lust for life and becoming a role model for others and an asset to his community.

Kim Joss

Chapter Eight

Kim is an inspiring entrepreneur, empower mentor, health coach and cancer victor who built a successful organization from rock bottom during a challenging time in her life. She discovered the power and purpose in self love and healing through whole body health, wellness, proper nutrition, supplementation and surroundings. Through this shift, and what she has overcome, Kim now finds herself living authentically and abundantly alongside her two children, husband and two dogs. She supports her clients to experience their big best life.

To connect or for more information about or how you can work with Kim:

https://www.facebook.com/kimm.joss or healyoursoulself@gmail.com

Elli Petrovska

Chapter Nine

Elli Petrovska lives in Sydney, Australia with her family. From early on and to this day, she has always been known as the "different one" among her family and friends as she has always challenged her family, always dancing to a different beat against conformity.

As a seeker of knowledge and wisdom, Elli is self-motivated, ambitious, passionate and driven about her vision and purpose. Her intention is to lead by example in all the roles she play's in her life.

Elli is currently working in Corporate, however is following her purpose and is investing in property, reading and writing. She continues to travel around the world to experience different cultures and fulfil her life's goals.

Sandy Escabi

Chapter Ten

Sandy Escabi is originally from Bogotá - Colombia. Since she was a child the desire to help others was apparent, and she started teaching reading and writing to people in need.

She grow up in a traditional Latin environment, surrounded by love and support from the whole family, her father, mother and sister have an important role as a foundation for her formation over the years.

Sandy has a Master degree in Administration and Management of Educational Centers from Barcelona-

Spain, and a Bachelor Degree in Education from Iberoamerican University Bogotá - Colombia where she collaborated in writing the book "La Enseñanza en el Pensamiento de Vives y Comenius" in 1997.

She has 20 years of experience as a Spanish Instructor at the post-secondary and elementary school levels. While at Seminole Community College and other schools, Sandy developed their curriculum for the Spanish program.

She understands the importance of a curriculum that supports language fluency as a student progresses through Spanish classes in Middle School, High School and Adult levels.

Sandy lives in the United States where she continues with her journey welcoming new possibilities, loving her family, helping others, and grateful for each moment and chapter in her life.

Nikki Galagher

Chapter Eleven

Nikki Galagher has worked in many industries while trying to find her passion and what makes her heart sing.

She has worked...

* In hospitality in multiple pubs, hotels and restaurants.

* Taught in a hospitality college.

* Sales and support for Gray Line a day tour company.

* Spray tanner in a beauty salon.

* Sales and member support manager for 21st Century Education, a financial education company, also events and logistics.

* Fashion stylist and sales assistant for City Chic a plus size clothing store.

* And now her passion - online business which is 90% automated where Nikki helps people become healthy and wealthy and changing lives in ways she never dreamed was possible.

She is a six time brain surgery survivor, a student of life - constantly learning and growing, grateful for so many things, experiences and people in her life. Vegan and on a quest to live a healthy, happy life and treat her body like the temple that it is.

Nikki Galagher

www.nikkigalagher.com

www.nikkiblu.com

Afterword

I hope you enjoyed the collection of heart felt stories, wisdom and vulnerability shared. Story telling is the oldest form of communication and I hope you feel inspired to take a step to living a fulfilling life. Feel free to contact any of the authors in this book or the other books in this series.

Part of the proceeds of this book, will go to the Bali Street Kids Project, in Denpasar, Bali.

The project gives orphaned and abandoned children a home, meals and an education.

You can donate to this amazing cause here: http://ykpa.org/

Other books in the series are...

Finding Inspiration: A Journey Of Riches, Book Eleven

https://www.amazon.com/dp/B07F1LS1ZW

Building your Life from Rock Bottom: A Journey Of Riches, Book Ten

https://www.amazon.com/Building-your-Life-Rock-Bottom-ebook/dp/B07CZK155Z?pd_rd_wg=QoVt3&pd_rd_r=21874ec8-c199-43a0-9f7c-6b37a2c5cb86&pd_rd_w=BHfGz&ref

Transformation Calling: A Journey Of Riches, Book Nine

https://www.amazon.com/Transformation-Calling-Journey-John-Spender-ebook/dp/B07BWQY9FB/

Letting Go and Embracing the New: A Journey Of Riches, Book Eight

https://www.amazon.com/Letting-Go-Embracing-New-Journey/dp/0648284506/

Making Empowering Choices: A Journey Of Riches, Book Seven

https://www.amazon.com/Making-Empowering-Choices-Journey-Riches-ebook/dp/B078JXMK5V

The Benefit of Challenge: A Journey Of Riches, Book Six

https://www.amazon.com/Benefit-Challenge-Journey-Riches-ebook/dp/B0778S2VBD/

Personal Changes: A Journey Of Riches, Book Five

https://www.amazon.com/Personal-Changes-Journey-John-Spender-ebook/dp/B075WCQM4N/

Dealing with Changes in Life: A Journey Of Riches, Book Four

https://www.amazon.com/Dealing-Changes-Life-Motivational-Inspirational-ebook/dp/B0716RDKK7/

Making Changes: A Journey Of Riches, Book Three

https://www.amazon.com/Making-Changes-Journey-changes-Spiritual-ebook/dp/B01MYWNI5A/

The Gift In Challenge: A Journey Of Riches, Book Two

https://www.amazon.com/Gift-Challenge-Self-Help-Anthology-Spiritual-ebook/dp/B01GBEML4G/

From Darkness into the Light: A Journey Of Riches, Book One

https://www.amazon.com/Darkness-into-Light-Motivation-Inspiration-ebook/dp/B018QMPHJW/

Thank you to all the authors that have shared aspects of their lives in the hope that it will inspire others to live a bigger version of themselves. I heard a great saying from Jim Rohan **"You can't complain and feel grateful at the same time"** at any given moment we have a chose to either feel like a victim of life or connected and grateful for it. I hope this book helps you to feel grateful go after your dreams.

www.ingramcontent.com/pod-product-compliance
Lightning Source LLC
Chambersburg PA
CBHW071902290426
44110CB00013B/1241